FOREVER FRANCIE

FOREVER FRANCIE

MY LIFE WITH JACK MILROY

MARY LEE

BLACK & WHITE PUBLISHING

First published 2005
by Black & White Publishing Ltd
99 Giles Street, Edinburgh, Scotland

ISBN 1 84502 070 7

Copyright © Mary Lee Milroy 2005

British Library Cataloguing in Publication Data:
A catalogue record for this book is available
from the British Library.

Printed and bound by Creative Print & Design Group

CONTENTS

ACKNOWLEDGEMENTS

My thanks to journalist Lesley Hardie for her invaluable help with this book and for her friendship.

My thanks also to Mae Burnside, my hairdresser, for keeping me lookin' good and for her friendship.

DEDICATION

To Ross, Ryan, Darrel, Adrian
Rebecca and Lilly Mae

PROLOGUE

What a star studded magical evening. It was truly one of the highlights of our long theatrical career – the Royal Scottish Variety Performance in the presence of their Royal Highnesses the Prince and Princess of Wales. It was the evening of Sunday, October 2, 1983 at the King's Theatre in Glasgow, and I'm happy to say it was during the young Royal couple's happiest times.

What excitement. I looked at the beautiful programme and there we were in all our glory – 'Jack Milroy and Mary Lee.'

After a long and nail-biting wait, Jack and I eventually hit the stage with our funnies, both dressed to the hilt. Jack pretended to throw a mousetrap into the Royal Box, saying, 'There's someone in there who is married to a man who cannot keep his trap shut'. At that time, Prince Charles was doing all the talking.

Later, when we were being presented backstage, Princess Diana said to Jack, 'You should REALLY have thrown the mousetrap. I was always a good catcher at school.'

And turning to me, she asked, 'Are you really married to him?'

'Yes, Ma'am,' I said. 'And I've got two nice kids to prove it.'

Diana was a charming young girl, but not as shy as she appeared to be.

Prince Charles spoke to Jimmy Logan's sister Annie Ross, the jazz singer. He looked at her extremely high heeled shoes and remarked, 'How do you walk in those?'

To which Annie not unreasonably replied, 'With great difficulty, Sir.'

He then moved down the presenting line to comic Hector Nicol and said, 'I liked your stretcher gag.'

Hector replied, 'Do you mean the one that goes "Never make love on a stretcher, 'cos you might get carried away"?'

Prince Charles laughed and said he'd use the line . . . and I do hope he did.

We ended an unforgettable evening being wined and dined and rubbing shoulders with the great and the good and I found myself thinking how fortunate we were to have come so far from our humble beginnings in Kinning Park and Shawlands in Glasgow.

Jack always laughed and said that Shawlands was a cut above me and I think he was right. In Kinning Park in the Thirties they used to say if a cat had a tail it was a tourist! Nevertheless, I feel that our formative childhood years did us no harm. On the contrary, our upbringing probably made us the sturdy survivors we both became and I can remember so much of it . . . as if it were only yesterday.

1
LOOK MA, I'M SINGING

I was born in a second floor tenement flat in Scotland Street, Kinning Park, Glasgow. Named Mary Ann, I was the first born to Isa and Willie McDevitt. My brother Eddie was born three and a half years after me, and my mother idolised him from the day he was born till the day she was no more.

My childhood was a happy one. We lived in a room and kitchen, but we had an inside 'lavvy'. We were toffs! Of course, these were much simpler times but we always had plenty to do. One of my favourite things at home was our little wireless set and I'd often go behind it and sing to whatever band was playing on the radio. 'Look Ma, I'm singing,' I'd say. Performing was a natural part of me from a very early age.

We also had an upright piano squeezed into our little flat and I took lessons at the house of a formidable woman who lit her piano with candles. It must have saved on the electricity but it was a wee bit spooky. And if I played a wrong note, she'd whack a sharp cane over my fingers.

During term time there would be no-one at home when I got back from school so I'd let myself in by putting my hand through the letterbox to retrieve the key, which was hanging on a long piece of string. Then I'd change into my play clothes, go into the kitchen and have a piece and jam – white bread with thick jam on top – and then go into the only other room in the flat to get on with my piano practice and see if I could avoid the cane at my next lesson.

I'd start with the best of intentions, but as I played I'd slowly begin to jazz the piece up. Where this talent came from, don't ask me, but 'The Bluebells of Scotland' were being swung, that's for sure.

The dyke in the back court was my first stage. I'd shout, 'Open your windows, Mary McDevitt's going to do a show' and my pals and I would dress up in crepe paper, then dance and sing to our hearts' delight.

Incidentally, my piano lessons weren't a waste of money. When I attended Scotland Street Primary School, now a Charles Rennie Mackintosh Museum, I used to play the school piano as the children marched to their classroom after morning prayers. And little did I know that I was hanging up my wee coat on a Mackintosh peg!

Many years later, Jack and I were driving past the Scotland Street school and he turned to me and said, 'Would you like to have a wee look at your old school?' I said I would, and in we trotted, only to find that they were celebrating V.E. Day. There was a crowd of people dressed in wartime costumes and singing along to wartime songs. As soon as we were in the door the curator recognised me and said, 'Come on, Mary, give us a song'. And I did. I gave them 'A Nightingale Sang in Berkeley Square' and when I finished, the curator kindly took us round the school and we reminisced about my school days.

The first thing I recalled was the cookery class with its old-fashioned stove and a big kettle sitting on it waiting to be boiled. How the memories came flooding back.

But it wasn't all good. If we misbehaved we'd get the strap, but it was just part of normal school life and we all simply accepted it. I took great pride in not crying – that would have let the side down.

The only people who frightened me at school were the

bullies. The worst of them were two big girls who were forever picking on me. I used to dread it when they'd come up to me and say menacingly, 'I'll see you at four.' Terrified, I'd run all the way home, in the close and up the stairs as fast as my wee legs would carry me.

Sometimes the heavy mob would come to the door later on with shouts of, 'I'll get you.' But by then, with my mother at home, I'd fearlessly shout back, 'Aye, if I let you.'

The streets and playground had strict rules and we stuck to them.

My father, known affectionately as 'Wullie', was a hard working man, very handsome, with a shock of beautiful black hair. His wage as a lorry driver with Shell Mex was £3 and ten shillings a week, and that was to keep the four of us. He was a mild-mannered man, but if we took liberties with him and roused his anger then it was straight under the bed to hide for my brother and me. In our wee flat that was the only hiding place so he knew exactly where to look for us. If we'd really made him angry then he'd pull us out by the feet and give us two of the best.

We respected our parents and always knew exactly where we stood with them. If you did wrong, you paid the price.

Down the street from our tenement lived my Granny Barbour, my mother's mum. We always got on well and I think my love of singing came from her. I loved going to see Gran and my favourite chore each night was to take some dinner down to her – usually some soup in a can. It was an old-fashioned can with a handle and if you swung it round your head quickly enough you didn't spill a drop.

There was a chapel on the way down to my gran's house, and one night I laid the can down and stotted my ball which went into the gutter. I picked it up and washed it in holy water at the entrance to the chapel. The priest caught me, and wasn't best pleased.

I always had my mother's undivided attention on a Sunday morning. She'd polish my shoes, put out clean socks, my good dress, coat and hat, and off we'd go to church. Curiously, I don't recall my father or brother coming with us. But I loved going to church and feeling that sense of occasion which we didn't get in our daily lives. It always made me feel like a toff.

After my time at Scotland Street Primary School I went on to Lambhill Street School after sitting the qualifying exam. You went in at 11 and left school at 14. I loved my time there, learning typing, bookkeeping and shorthand. And I used to jazz up the typewriter to keep myself amused!

It was around this time that I began to take my singing and impressions more seriously. Up till then I had always wanted to be a hairdresser and often burned my pals' hair with the old fashioned tongs you held over a flame to heat, but singing was starting to bring in a little money each week which was like manna from heaven to my mother. Our family needed all the money we could get.

My dad would take me to all my wee concerts. From the proceeds he'd get a packet of fags and I'd get a bar of chocolate. The rest went into the household kitty. What talent I had was God-given. I was a natural jazz singer which was a big surprise to me then, but not anymore. All the best jazz singers are either Scottish or American. It must be something in the brown bread!

As well as singing, I did impressions of Maurice Chevalier and Gracie Fields, two of the biggest stars of those days. I suppose I must have seen them on my mid-week trips to the pictures with my mother and they were both fabulous enter-tainers.

While I'd have my eyes glued to the screen, Mother would get into her seat in the stalls and in a few minutes she'd be fast asleep. I'd nudge her and say, 'Why do you come to the pictures if you always fall asleep?'

She would reply, 'Mary, this is the best wee sleep I get all week, with nobody asking me to make the tea.'

We didn't call it the cinema. We called it 'the pictures', and a rare night it was – two big pictures and a Pathe Gazette newsreel. The only time you saw royalty was on the news at the pictures – Queen Mary with her toque hat and King George with his splendid naval headgear.

We lived in a different world from today's, but oh, so much happier.

Another important influence on my childhood was Auntie Honor, my mother's lifelong friend. I remember being taken to her house on a Saturday night for my tea. When the meal was finished, we children were sat up on a long sideboard and the mothers and fathers all did the Charleston to the music of an old 'caw the haundle' gramophone.

I loved watching them. It was a real rave to me!

At home in the tenement, the hole-in-the-wall bed was well used. My brother and I slept in the double bed and my mother's father, Grandpa Barbour, in the aforementioned.

He gave Eddie and me no aggro because he was very deaf, so we would blether away at nights and never annoyed him. There was a wee curtain he could pull across to give him privacy.

Grandpa Barbour was a nice old man and my mother and her sister were brought up by him. I can see him even now, sitting at the kitchen fire in his favourite seat, with a tartan blanket over his knees.

A baker to trade, he had an early rise and was always early to bed. When my mother was a bit older, she used to go to the all-night 'jiggin'. The women paid a penny to get in, and if she didn't fancy the talent in one hall, Mum would jump on a tram car to the next dance hall and get home around 4am.

When she finally got home, Grandpa would shout, 'What time is it Isa?' and she'd say, 'Midnight, Father.' It kept him happy! My mother would then open the kitchen window and hang her head out, in case she fell asleep, because there was no time for that. She and her faithful pal Honor met at 6.30am to catch the Govan Ferry across the River Clyde to get to work. They slept all the way over and when she was packing her biscuits at Bilslands biscuit factory, Mum could still hear the sound of the Eightsome Reel ringing in her ears as she worked.

When life grew much better for me, I lived in the same block of flats as Lady Bilsland and I used to think to myself, 'My Mammy packed your biscuits!' I didn't mention it to her though!

At that time we knew so little of things medical, but looking back, it may well be that Grandpa Barbour suffered from Alzheimer's Disease. I can only surmise, but when he went to collect his pension Mum would say to me, 'Keep an eye on him, but don't let him see you watching.'

Sometimes he'd get up to go to the loo and go back to the wrong bed. My brother and I had a great laugh at that, but the old soul was losing the place. Eventually, it got too much for my mother to cope with and, one day, I came home from school and saw an ambulance at the close. My mother was crying and it was horrible. I slid into a corner, and put my hands over my ears to blot out my Grandpa's shouts. I knew that our lives were going to change from that day on, and they did.

He died two months later, and I'd plead with my mother to keep the light on when it was time for sleep. I'd explain, 'It's my Grandpa's photo, he's staring at me.' The offending photograph had to come off the wall. He was my pal in life, but I was scared to look at his face when he'd gone.

I think my mother put my school photograph up instead, and things gradually returned to normal. But my, did I miss my Saturday penny and my Grandpa's comforting presence around the house.

Thinking back to those days, my childhood was so innocent. There was no television, no internet, no mobile phones. We had the freedom to enjoy going out to play with pals and games like peaver, kick the can, rounders and skipping were all played outside in the street. And yet we had much more responsibility at an early age than today's children. We grew up smartish and started work in the real world at fourteen years of age. And looking back, I'm sure we had the best of it.

2

MASTER 'MAKE DOWNS'

Jack Milroy was born at 103 Coplaw Street in Govanhill. We had very similar upbringings and when we got to know each other we discovered great parallels in our childhoods.

At the top end of his street was the famous Tramway Depot, where at 5 o'clock every morning, hundreds of trams trundled out to service the city of Glasgow. At the bottom end was the very busy and exciting shopping area of Cathcart Road.

Halfway between the two was their house, facing a little square play park. Jack lived in the top flat in the tenement building, with a front room and a back room which was the kitchen. Both rooms had a hole-in-the-wall bed and like us they had an inside toilet, which of course was real luxury in those days.

From what Jack told me they were a happy family. He was the middle one of three brothers. The first born, Tommy, was very clever. Andrew, the younger, was very artistic, and he had the sweetest little sister, Cathie.

Jack's mother Mary used to say, 'I've got three kids and one I'm not sure about.' That was the self-invented Jack Milroy, who was born James Cruden, to Mary and David Cruden.

Jack said his mother was a gem. She was the dominant one in the marriage, very self-sufficient. And by God she had to be. She was widowed at an early age and the years that followed must have been very hard for her.

She had arrived in Scotland from the South of Ireland at the age of 12 when her folks had sent her to Glasgow to stay with relatives and find a job. She soon started in domestic service as a 'teenie weenie' working in big houses in Glasgow for the toffs, as she used to call them. She worked upstairs downstairs and had a uniform and a bed, 'all found', and a wage of 7/6d a month. It was a hard life for a young girl but one of her favourite jobs was going down to the family holiday house in Helensburgh, on the coast, to warm it up before the toffs arrived to spend their summer holiday.

Jack's only regret about his relationship with his mother was that when he came out of the army he never took his mum away for the little holidays she would have loved so much, but then the young mind didn't work that way. There were always too many other things going on.

Jack's father was a master wood carver and worked for R&T Jackson in Darnley Street in Glasgow. I didn't have the good fortune to know him, as he had passed on before I met Jack, but Jack adored him and told me he was a very mild, charming man, whose family meant everything to him. As was the fashion at the time, he liked to wear a bowler hat and a high collar, very spruce. But he was a real family man and a dedicated father and loved nothing better than spending time with his kids and tucking into his wife's rice puddings with sultanas on the top.

His father's work was a joy to behold. He made ball and claw legs for chairs and carved roses and various flowers on wardrobe doors. He was a real artist.

Jack vividly remembered that the family had one of the very early radios, called a 'cat's whiskers' and it was his father's pride and joy. To get a better reception, his father would wrap the wires round the bath tap. Jack and his brothers would then sneak in and loosen them and giggle at their dad's annoyance at the poor quality of the sound . . . funny the things you remember.

11

Jack's first school was St. John Cuthbertson's Primary. It was at the top of Coplaw Street, just before the Tramway Depot and as it was only two minutes from his house it was very handy.

Everybody had a nickname and Jack was saddled with 'Make Downs', because his clothes were re-fashioned to fit him when his brother Tommy grew out of them. It was a cruel name, and the memory of it still upset Jack years later, though he could laugh about the time his mother bought herself a purple suit jacket and skirt. She obviously didn't care for it, and decided to do a 'remodelling' job on it but not for herself. The next day Jack was to go to school wearing a purple jacket and short purple pants. It was a nightmare, and he refused to go, cried and made a real fuss, but had to put it on. Well, with the tantrums, he was very late for school, and ran like the clappers up Coplaw Street. It was a horrible day, lashing with rain, and in his hurry he tripped in the road and fell flat on his face in a dirty great puddle. So back he went to the house. His mother was angry, but she relented, let Jack change into his other school suit . . . and the purple one was never seen again, much to his relief.

Jack often talked about the good times, too, when the summer break was approaching . . . and the school picnics which were always a firm favourite. Everybody clambered on to a horse and cart and the kids sat with their classmates, each with a tin mug on a piece of string hung round their necks and a label stating their name and what class they were in. They would make for the nearest green space, which was Queens Park and spend the day running races, enjoying the picnic and having a wee giggle with the girls in their class.

Then came the long awaited summer break. Oh glory, what joy and fun, running about the street in your bare feet and following the water cart and feeling nice and cool with your feet soaked in the spray. The tar on the roads used to bubble in the heat. Jack and I had great memories of our childhood summers and the summers years ago seemed so much better.

When he left primary school Jack went on to Shawlands Academy, and left school aged 14. That wasn't a problem in those days. In fact, it was what most people did. There was plenty of work then and all his pals were employed within two or three days of leaving school.

Jack found work as an office boy and worked for three years with Dundas Hamilton, a Glasgow insurance brokers firm. Every day he travelled by the 'puggy circle' (the Cathcart Circle) but he then moved on to Osborne Garretts in Bothwell Street, a company which supplied hairdressing salon equipment.

Like me, during all this time, Jack was keen on entertaining. He said he thought it went back to the time he was ten and would go with his father to the Queens Park on a Sunday to see the show laid on in the bandstand. It must have struck a chord somewhere within him and sowed the seeds of his future.

Jack's dad was happy taking him along to see the shows and when he was about 15 they moved on to proper theatres. Their favourite venue was the Coliseum where you could see shows for a 6d ticket from the gallery – a real bargain. They both loved the long chorus line – a show just wasn't a show without it – and his dad particularly enjoyed it when there was a large company on stage to entertain him.

When he was a young teenager, Jack would go with his pals on a Sunday afternoon to a coffee shop in Minard Road, for a coffee and a Jacobs Club biscuit . . . heaven! And it was a great way to get an audience. With an exuberance he retained all his life, Jack would stand on his head and tell jokes. Not so easy to do!

He reckoned he got his love of theatre from his father, and his sense of humour from his mother, who was good at telling jokes and was always a riot when she went to the local shops. And it wasn't long before the lure of the stage was too much to resist.

The Locarno dance hall in Sauchiehall Street held regular competitions for newcomers and amateur entertainers and one day Jack saw a sign saying 'non-winner's fare paid'. That was good enough for him and off he went for his first try at the stage. He won a place in the final.

His tap dancing routine had been practised and honed at the 'close mouth' (the entrance to the tenement block). He was self-taught, and when he was a kid he would put his hands against the wall and tap away. Then he improvised and made himself a tap mat out of a piece of venetian blind wrapped round an old mat and would go to competitions with it rolled up in brown paper under his arm.

Fred Astaire and Ginger Rogers were big stars on the cinema screen and inspired Jack and gave him plenty of material to try and copy. He was also a fan of the Nicholas Brothers, famous black Americans who were a fabulous tap dancing act. A long time later, when Jack became famous, he was presented with a professional tap mat by Scottish Ballet. They last forever . . . imagine that!

Jack won that Locarno competition with a song and a tap dance, and his prize was the princely sum of £10. He gave his mother £5, which was a bit of a surprise to her as Jack was only earning about £2 a week at the time. When she asked where he had got it, he told her he had entered the Locarno competition and won it. Half the time she didn't know what he was getting up to. Have tap mat, will travel. It was the start of Jack's long road to stardom.

3

SHOWBIZ – HERE I COME!

I was 13 when I read in the local evening paper 'Personality girl wanted to appear in a competition to be held at the Glasgow Empire Theatre'.

The auditions were held in the restaurant of the very elegant Pettigrew & Stephens department store in town. Roy Fox, the famous band leader of the Thirties, was in charge. An American, he broadcast from his permanent engagement at the famous Café de Paris in London and had found much fame and popularity both in the capital and on tour with his fabulous orchestra.

I immediately thought, 'This is for me.' I plunked school that afternoon and took the tram to Pettigrew & Stephens.

There was a fine pianist there to help us out. I sang 'My Kid's a Crooner', and just when I thought, 'I'd better get home or my mother will have a charlie,' a man called Leslie MacDonnell shouted, 'Mary McDevitt, will you please come and have a chat.'

When he asked how old I was I lied and said I was 14, the age you had to be to enter the competition. He asked me to come to the final that Friday night in the Empire Theatre, and to bring my parents along. When I rushed home and told my mother what I'd been up to she said, 'What's the prize?' When I told her it was five guineas, she said, 'Sit down and have something to eat.'

The excitement on the big night was intense. I wore a blue taffeta dress with long sleeves. The whole family came along, and I won the competition. Five guineas, a fortune to the McDevitts!

As we were getting ready to go home, the orchestra manager came and astonished my parents by asking permission for their daughter to join the orchestra on a permanent basis.

My father had to confess that his daughter would not be available until the 13th of August, my fourteenth birthday. They were very understanding and promised to send for me after the band's annual holiday in September. I don't think it sunk in to me that I was being offered the opportunity of a lifetime. I suppose I didn't really understand how it all worked at that time and I remember saying to my mother, 'Ach, I bet they forget all about me.'

When I left school in June I still had no word from the big band world, so I set about using my skills in typing and book-keeping to land a job in a slaters' office. My wage was 7/6d a week. But I was now bringing in three times that amount with my singing jobs and doing quite well.

One of the most enjoyable jobs I had was on a Saturday night with a local band led by Collie Shaw. I'd belt out numbers like 'Love in Bloom'. It was tough on the voice, but I loved every minute of it.

And I had my secret weapon. From the age of ten, I had started singing on Saturday nights at the church hall, and my Dad had a megaphone made for me. No microphones in those days and it really helped me to save my voice.

My job was a revelation. The slaters brought back so much mud and dirt on their boots that the office floor was always filthy. I couldn't stand the mess and used to pinch my mothers' soap and wash the floor every day.

Years later an old man stopped me in the street and said, 'Do you know me lassie? I was your boss in the slaters' office. You made a rare job of my floor.' Such is fame!

Then one day it happened. A telegram arrived asking me to join the Roy Fox Orchestra at the Streatham Locarno ballroom in London at the end of the month. I jumped for joy.

I had to be chaperoned, of course. My parents chose a charming lady, Alice Balnave, to accompany me on my travels. She had spent two years in America, and my mother reckoned Alice knew the ways of the world. Alice, my dad and I made the train journey to London. But he had work the next day and had to jump on to the first train back to Glasgow.

Dad didn't see my debut. In fact he didn't see me perform with the Roy Fox Orchestra until I returned in triumph to the Glasgow Empire Theatre, six months later.

The orchestra had arranged an all-inclusive contract with my parents. It meant I was not paid extra for recording sessions, late night dances or Sunday concerts. Instead, I was to get £5 per week for the first year, £6 for the second, and £7 for the third year. I did have perks like travelling expenses and my stage clothes but it wasn't really a lot to live on. Understandably, my parents were innocent in the ways of business.

The orchestra didn't pay Alice, so we both lived on £5 a week, and I also sent something home to my mum every week. Our life on the road was anything but glamorous but you could get theatrical digs for £1 a week with full board. In Woolworths in those days, nothing cost more than 6d. Betty-Lou powder and lipstick could be yours for 3d each. I suppose it's all comparative, but don't ask me how we survived!

Everybody looked on me as a star, which I was. It was a golden start to a show business career, but I can honestly say I never made any money in the three years I spent with the Orchestra. I wasn't unhappy, but I made sure I didn't sign any future contracts without reading the small print!

My first sight of the band in full flight was wonderful. It was at the Streatham Locarno in London. The band boys looked imposing in white jackets and black trousers. Roy Fox was immaculate, dressed in full tails from Savile Row. Known as 'the whispering trumpeter', he had great charm. And what a lifestyle his fame and fortune afforded him. He had a Rolls Royce, dined in the best restaurants and even had his own pedigree racehorse, named 'Whispering' after his famous signature tune.

The music was brilliant. He had the finest musicians in the country, a thirty-piece orchestra, and the sound was beautiful.

I was indeed in fairyland.

At one point during that first evening, Roy looked round at us and waved.

I said, 'Alice, he saw us, he saw us.' How innocent we were, two lambs to the slaughter. After the show, Alice and I went back to our digs in Streatham and fell asleep in a bed which had a plaque above it saying 'Bless This House'.

I cried myself to sleep.

In the morning we had a kipper for breakfast then dressed and went to rehearsal. I was to perform with the band that night but when I saw Roy Fox I said, 'I want to go home.' That was before I even put a foot on the stage! He was his usual charming self, however, and before I knew it we were rehearsing 'South American Joe.'

Though I cried myself to sleep with homesickness initially, after three weeks singing with this wonderful orchestra, I had no wish to go home. I was hooked on show business for the rest of my life.

My chaperone and I travelled from place to place on an enormous coach, rented to take the bands' instruments from town to town. Our pal was Barry the band boy, whose job was to look after all the instruments and set them up at the next theatre ready for the orchestra.

We were a happy threesome.

Alice and I ate in cheap cafes to sustain us for the trek round the next town to look for digs. We got used to this way of life. You can get used to anything when you are young. I lived for the show at night, when I would get into my pretty stage outfit, a white satin long-sleeved blouse and black satin trousers, which blended in nicely with the band boys' black and white suits.

And I got a new name. Mary McDevitt doesn't exactly jump out at you from a marquee, so I was called Mary-lee – short, sweet and easily remembered. Roy Fox always announced me as 'Little Mary Lee', and it became my trademark.

I had never had a professional singing lesson in my life and Roy Fox never told me how to sing a song. He let me do it my way, and it seemed to work. He did tell the band boys *not* to play me Peggy Lee or Ella Fitzgerald records in case I'd copy their phrasing and lose my own. Sound advice for any young singer.

Being young and not very tall, I had to stand on a wooden box to reach the 'mike'. But one lesson I soon learned was that the microphone was my best friend. When I watch recording artists of today it's not so different, just a bit more digital and high-tech. That's progress.

The first broadcast I made, I produced all my stage actions to a bare wall and the band boys laughed heartily at my antics. We recorded at St. John's Wood Studios in London most of the time and during breaks in the session the band would get themselves a coffee. Alice and I would stay put and read our magazines. We simply didn't have the money for a coffee.

The band boys were much better paid than I was. They all had nice cars to travel in and when we weren't recording I didn't see much of them during the day. I learned later they were told never, under any circumstances, to swear in front of me or tell unsavoury stories, and to treat me with the utmost respect, so it was little wonder that they kept out of my way.

Touring days had a routine. Each Monday morning I'd get

dressed in my tatty digs then Alice and I would report to the theatre for a publicity stunt. Then we would join Roy for lunch, whisked off in his Rolls Royce to the finest restaurants in town. Roy Fox taught me the refinements of good living.

The first time this happened I stared at the huge array of cutlery, not knowing which to pick up. My mentor whispered, 'Start from the outside, honey.' It was sore, but I learned the finer points of life during my £5-a-week year.

What I missed in good honest fun with my Kinning Park pals could never have made up for the school of life I was so unceremoniously flung into at such an early age. Thank goodness I was a quick learner.

Mind you, I often think I missed out a lot of my natural growing up years. I used to sit on the bandstand at dances, and ache to get down onto the dance floor to do the jitterbug. And I had to put up with all the girls gazing adoringly at the band boys. I honestly don't remember anyone gazing adoringly at me!

On my first visit back to the Glasgow Empire with the band, my family was still living in the elastic wee room and kitchen. I remember asking my mother to put out a butter knife for me as she set the table for a meal! She must have thought I was a right wee upstart, but she said nothing, though I think she breathed a sigh of relief when the week was over. I had changed, which was only natural, and the wee room and kitchen was a far cry from taking tea at the Savoy!

A reporter from the local paper came to interview my family and get their thoughts on my success. My wee brother remarked on my absence by saying, 'It's like having twelve people out of the house.' He took all the fuss in his stride, but for the rest of his life he called me 'Miss Lee'.

4

A TRIUMPHANT HOMECOMING
AND SOME NUT HOUSE CAPERS!

At the start of my first ever week at the Glasgow Empire, my folks ordered a taxi to take me to the theatre each evening. There must have been 100 people waiting at the close to see the local girl star going to work. What they didn't know was that my father stopped the taxi at Paisley Road Toll and we continued the journey by bus, because we couldn't afford the fare into town.

When we arrived at the Empire there was always a queue of people waiting to see me at the stage door, and I happily signed their autograph books for them. This didn't happen at every theatre but it was a big occasion for me and the Glasgow folk. They were the salt of the earth, waiting to applaud their own 'Little Mary Lee.' So, I was skint but famous. It could have been worse.

I had a nightly ritual at the theatre with the always immaculate Mr. Fox. Before the performance each evening I had to knock on his dressing room door. It was similar to having an audience with God – he was such a remote figure to me. He would say, 'Come in, baby,' then I had to twirl around to assure him I was perfectly groomed for the show.

He always looked at my hands and said, 'Still biting your nails, honey.'

I never could stop that bad habit till, one Christmas, I received 12 manicure sets from the band boys. Needless to say, I have never bitten my nails since.

I made my entrance each night during that week at the Empire to wonderful applause and sang 'South American Joe' and a couple of swingy choruses with The Cubs, a fine vocal group who backed my numbers. Things were going well, so well that the 1937 'Melody Maker' annual poll for readers to choose their favourites made me Best Girl Singer, with Vera Lynn second. Nobody told me officially that I had won. One of the band boys let it slip. Maybe Roy Fox thought I'd ask for more money if he told me! It was just another day, and I didn't even get a box of chocolates.

I soon forgot about my accolade. In fact it was many years later before I realised the honour the public had paid me. I was happy to be 'Little Mary Lee,' belting out my jazz numbers and enjoying the many little gems that were to come to me during my years with this fantastic orchestra.

When the band was booked to play in Brussels, I had to have an interview with a magistrate as I was under 18, then the legal age to travel abroad on your own without legitimate proof of being cared for. Off we went, Alice and I and the Orchestra, on our first trip abroad to perform. I loved Brussels, even though we had to do seven days a week and three shows a day. Exciting but exhausting.

Another interesting occasion was my first encounter with royalty. Alice and I arrived that day to do an afternoon show in a West End theatre and I remember I was summoned to the Master's presence and he carefully showed me how I should bow to the audience, to the box, and back to the audience.

No one told me why, but when I had finished singing, I did as I had been told. When I looked up I saw what to me was just an old woman sitting with her pal, wearing the most enormous toque hat. Later one of the band boys said, 'Did you not see Queen Mary?' (the present Queen's granny). I don't think I was particularly impressed at the time, but I never forgot the occasion.

Another gem springs to mind. It was 1937 and this time the destination was Alexandra Palace in London, the original home of television. I was made up in a tiny dressing room and some awful yellow stuff was applied to my face. There were only two little studios, and the announcer was a charming lady called Jasmine Blye. I sang my song to the camera then belted outside for a picnic. There were miles of fields around and I remember it was a fun day. In those days the radius of television was about ten miles, so it was only those and such as those who thought of having a television set. The BIG thing then was radio, and we did plenty of that.

We recorded shows for Radio Luxembourg, done after the show at night on the stage where we were playing but it was all just part of the job.

By 1938 I was coming to my third year – the £7-a-week year – with the orchestra. It was a happy time. We did the Moss Empire circuit and got to know most of the finest acts in the country, names like Jimmy Wheeler, and Bartlet and Ross, female impersonators who took off their wigs at the end of their act – it was the law in those days. And the famous Wilson, Keppel and Betty, of course, doing their sand dance.

I didn't get to know the acts well as I had to stay in my dressing room until the band show, but if I went to the theatre during the day to collect mail there would be jugglers perfecting their act and dancers shining up their routines, and they would teach me what to do. So I learned to juggle and dance, and learned the tricks of an acrobatic act, too – which all stood me in good stead in later years.

Our annual holiday was always the entire month of August, and 1938 was no different. Alice and I arrived home and my mother took a wee room and kitchen in Rothesay for the month. There was dancing on the front to a wee man playing the melodeon and I sat on the pier waiting to be asked to dance. But nobody recognised me offstage! I was not amused. There had even been a write-up in the local paper about the two stars on the island that summer, Jack Buchanan and Mary Lee. They forgot to mention that Jack was a guest of the Marquis of Bute, and I was in a room and kitchen up a back street. My mother had a good laugh though. 'Mary, you mix with the best,' she said.

Towards the end of this holiday, however, I received a telegram which was to change the pattern of my life forever. It said, 'Join Jack Payne's Orchestra at the end of August' and was sent by Leslie MacDonnell, Roy Fox's manager, who had now set himself up in management. This was a shock. I was perturbed because there had been no indication of the band disbanding when we broke up for the holidays. Always the practical one, my mother said, 'Ach well, you're lucky to have a job.'

I had joined Roy Fox in September 1935 and spent three of the happiest years of my life with his great orchestra. I was also groomed in every way – speech, dress, manners, you name it, I had it. We toured during the entire three years of my stay and made many records for Decca and HMV.

The good news was that Jack Payne's orchestra was equally famous. But what lay ahead? I was being flung into the big world on my own. No chaperone this time – Alice wanted to stay at home. This didn't really worry me as I thought I could look after myself perfectly well.

Trying to be practical, my first concern was money. I was adamant that nobody would take me for a fool. I had done my apprenticeship and paid my dues. When my new boss offered me £8 a week, I politely refused. He said that I was only getting £7 with Roy Fox, but I explained that I knew my worth now.

Well, he agreed, and I got my money.

My mother was delighted. 'Mary,' she said, 'Your daddy's never earned more than £4 a week in his life.' With my new found wealth, I was able to help her, and it wasn't long before she had moved to her big house in Hillington – 248 Talla Road to be precise.

My gentle, well-trained band boys with the Roy Fox Orchestra were a thing of the past. Jack Payne's boys viewed me as a mature girl, which I now was. I had to learn the hard way to keep them at arms' length, but the chase was interesting!

I hated being with Jack Payne's band. He treated you like nothing and only spoke to you through his manager. He had a plooky face and a bad temper. A world of difference from Roy Fox.

I sang 'A Tisket, A Tasket', one of Ella Fitzgerald's hits, with a great orchestration. Me and the band made great music together. But the manager said, 'Mr. Payne said to stop phrasing your number like Ella Fitzgerald.'

I'd never heard the woman sing it, so I didn't know how to change my style to suit him. We never gelled, and I was happy to leave his merry band after three months.

Luck was with me. I joined Jack Jackson's Band. What a joy that was! Jack, who was later to become one of our finest radio DJs, was a joy to work for, a big personality with a heart to match. I had a fun time, but unfortunately, I didn't record with either band. The only recording session I did in my own right was for Parlophone. I was accompanied by most of the Fox boys, in a special deal set up for me by Maurice Burman, the drummer, who had become a good friend.

I stayed with Jack for six months, then got restless and went back to London. I was tired of touring and just wanted to stay put for a while. I longed for a residency in London.

My lifeline at this time was a lady called Alma Warren, Maurice Burman's sister. With her then partner and boyfriend, Lord Ulick Brown, she co-owned a nightclub called The Nut

House. He was like an Adonis – tall, blond and sexy – and Alma had brains she hadn't even used yet. The girls came in to see Ulick, and the fellows paid the piper.

When I wasn't working I would phone Alma, and nine times out of ten she'd say, 'Start Monday, Mary.' It kept me going and was a good showcase for my work.

The Master of Ceremonies at the club was Al Burnett whose son Barry went on to become Barbara Windsor's agent. Al had stock gags like, 'The food is untouched by human hands. There are monkeys in the kitchen.' All clever stuff. Al later owned his own club, The Stork, in Regent Street.

The late Tommy Cooper played The Nut House long before he became famous, and did the same kind of act even then, with the fez and glasses. I used to watch him setting up his tricks backstage.

At The Nut House I learned that it was harder to entertain the elite than your average Joe. Lovely people when sober, but put the ear plugs in when they'd had a few!

But I loved my time there. It suited me just fine.

One night, Alma asked me to join a table of men to have a drink with them. Normally I never mixed with the guests and I declined because I didn't drink and I thought the request demeaning. We all knew there were hostesses to keep the boys happy. But she seemed determined to have me sit with these men, and mindful of her kindness to me, I obliged. I must say that they were charming company but before too long I took my leave of them to get ready for my show. It was a Friday, with a noisy audience and I was battering through one of my standards when the loudest voice you've ever heard shouted, 'Give the kid a chance.'

The whole room became silent. Only later did I realise my companions were members of the famous Messini Gang, a notorious bunch much feared in London.

Alma had another trick up her sleeve. She would invite the

principals of a West End musical to wine and dine. Later, when the cabaret started, she had the finest show in town. The only performer who didn't grace her cabaret floor was the late and great society entertainer Hutch. He took five bows then sat down to finish his meal – and good luck to him, I say.

Always on the lookout for something new to entertain her clientele, Alma engaged a stripper who was known as the finest exponent of her art. It was 1939, and Page 3 girls were light years away! I was a bit shocked and said I wasn't dressing with a lady who took her clothes off for a living. But I did, and a nicer girl I've yet to meet. Her mother stood at the side of the stage and when the act was over she'd put a cloak around her daughter's shoulders until they got back to the dressing room. She maintained her daughter's dignity.

One of my happiest weeks at the club was when I worked with a deputy pianist. When my own was ill, Alma came to the rescue and said that George would play for me. He and his brother used to come each evening and when the band took a break, George would go on and play beautifully. He was blind. When we got together he asked what keys I sang in and I told him what I wanted. We hit the stage, and I've never been accompanied so well before, or since.

His name was George Shearing, the jazz pianist who went on to be a star in America and Britain. Many years later, George was being interviewed on radio and he was asked which singers had influenced him most in his lifetime. He said that one was Mary Lee, an accolade indeed. I would never have known about his remarks if Maureen Beattie, delightful actress daughter of comedian Johnny Beattie, had not telephoned her father from London to tell him about my lovely mention.

5

JACK'S FIRST STEPS
UP THE SHOWBIZ LADDER

Around 1938 Jack joined the amateur Pantheon Club, which at that time included names like Molly Weir, Willie Joss and Eddie Fraser, who later became Head of Light Entertainment at BBC Scotland. One of the many productions Jack appeared in was 'Stand Up and Sing', the Jack Buchanan musical, which the club ran for a week in the Princess Theatre, now the Glasgow Citizens Theatre. It was a terrific thrill for Jack because he modelled himself on Jack Buchanan, whom he had watched with his father from the gallery of the Alhambra Theatre doing all the musicals. In those days they used to come to Glasgow first before they opened in London.

Jack loved Buchanan, who was from Helensburgh originally, and became a big, big star of course, always immaculate in top hat and tails, a style Jack enthusiastically emulated. And when the costumes for the Pantheon Club productions were sent up in hampers from London, Jack and a couple of mates would get dressed up and go down to Buchanan Street to a famous photographers there called Jerome's where you got three postcard-sized prints for a shilling. In their tails they looked like glamorous movie stars, but Jack's hat was so big that if it hadn't been for his ears it would have been over his face! By now, though, he knew he wanted his future to be on stage and screen. But how to go about it . . . there was the rub!

In the years leading up to the Second World War life for Jack was in turn hilarious, sad, bad and sometimes desperate, but always the optimist, he battled on. He hadn't a clue how to make showbiz a profession so he became a semi-professional, working during the day and doing odd concerts at night, appearing in town halls, tiny theatres, and Catholic concerts though he was a 'Proddy'.

In his later years, I used to listen to him regaling his fellow professionals with stories about his beginnings in show business. He looked back on his early start with great affection and laughed heartily. He had such a blessed nature.

I think he was on nodding terms with the unemployment exchange and was often on benefits. It suited him because he didn't want to be tied, so he wafted from one job to another because they were temporary and let him work away from home when the opportunity presented itself.

He chuckled when he told me about the time the labour exchange sent him to a maternity hospital to hang Christmas decorations. The women were tucked up in bed in the ward and when one woman saw Jack taking his decorations up the ladder she said, 'For God's sake son, don't slip. I'm just about to have my wean!' Jack's mother was black affronted when she heard where he had spent his afternoon. Most unsuitable!

His next job was working in a brewery and just after he started his boss said, 'Jack, just keep pumping up the barrel with your foot. I'll be back in a minute.' Poor Jack. When he took his foot away from the pump the place was flooded with beer and the boss didn't come back for three hours. The smell from his clothes displeased his mother, so she told him not to go back.

Plus the fact that he limped for a week.

Jack had another wee ploy around that time – selling electric irons for the Clydesdale Company at 2/6d per week. It must have been heartbreaking for him but his nature was always sunny, so I think that got him through the hard times. One thing was for sure – he wasn't going to be in an office for the rest of his days.

He had another wee job selling furniture, and he laughed when he told me that the older men always saw to it that HE carried the heavy end.

He was just about at the end of his tether with his daytime adventures when an agent called Stopher sent him up to the Highlands by bus, along with ten other performers, to entertain the men who were working on the ambitious Scottish Hydro Electric Board scheme of the time.

This was certainly not the 'crème de la crème' . . . no way. The accommodation was in tin huts and the theatre was not the best. It was winter and Jack was so cold he couldn't get to sleep.

One night they went off to do a show for the workers. As they drove to the venue the headlights of the bus lit up one of the lady performers struggling through the snow in full evening dress, clutching a half bottle of whisky to her chest. She had braved the elements to walk to the nearest pub.

As she got onto the bus she said to Jack, 'Is it no hellish what you have to do for a living?'

Jack took it all with a pinch of salt. After all, he was performing at night, learning how to cope with all kinds of audiences, the rough and the smooth.

At the end of one performance up north the promoter stepped forward and announced, 'Well boys, next week I've got a treat for you. I'm bringing up the world's strongest man, Hercules. He can pull two horses and a cart with his bare hands.'

A loud voice piped up from the audience, 'Never mind the horses. Get him to shift some of these bloody boulders!'

Another little gem Jack told was about the agent who used

Lauder's Bar in Sauchiehall Street as his office. He would book young comics and raw acts for 7/6d on a Sunday night. The pick up was a bus outside the pub. They all bought the agent a drink and duly turned up on Sunday, sometimes to be told, 'Sorry son, the bus is full. Come back next Sunday.'

But occasionally they'd get on the bus and off they'd go to strut their stuff at some little concert on the outskirts of Glasgow.

Jack's REAL entry into showbiz was an engagement with a gentleman called Dan Campbell. He toured little 'fit-up shows' around small villages, and Jack had to set up, sell tickets and do fly-posting. For young people, not a bad start.

Jack's wages were very small, but he was assured he was on five percent of any profit made over a certain sum.

Jack thought, 'This is it. I'm in the big time.'

He had very few stage clothes but one of the ladies in the company took him to Paddy's Market and got him a top hat and tails, a striped blazer and all the things he would need for the tour for the princely sum of five pounds.

Well, off they trotted, show at the ready. Weeks went by and all Jack got was the little wage, but ah, one week, he was informed that his five percent of the profit would be £10. He sent £5 to his mother and she sent back a telegram saying, 'Stick in son. Dumpling follows.'

That would be around the time she said, 'I've got two boys and one I'm not sure about.'

His family was quite artistic. His dad Davie drew the most beautiful sketches of 'Gaiety Girls', the chorus girls of his day. It must have rubbed off on Jack, the small beginnings of the comic genius that Jack Milroy was to become.

All in all though, these were hard days.

Although Jack always made you laugh when he recalled them, it must have been a relief in a way, when in 1940 he received his call-up papers to join the Black Watch and do his bit for King and Country.

6

AMBROSE AND ALL THAT JAZZ

Around this time, I was invited to do the Saturday night radio broadcasts from the Mayfair Hotel in London with Ambrose and his Orchestra. It was the top job but I was advised not to talk money to Ambrose but to wait and see what I would get at the end of each week in the sure knowledge that it would be plenty.

I rehearsed with the Ambrose band and was told to report to the Mayfair Hotel at 9pm, in good time for the late broadcast. But nobody told me which door to come in, so I floated through the main ballroom to reach the bandstand. Ambrose smiled at me, beckoned me onto the stand, then with venom whispered in my ear, 'Never do that again. Come through the kitchen like the rest of us.'

As the weeks went on, there was no sign of my enormous wages, so I decided the time had come to ask what was happening. I think Ambrose must have been in his gambling mode at this time because it took me three months to get my money, and when I eventually received the cheque, I realised I could have made more behind the counter at Woolworths!

It was another lesson well learned. Always get a contract and always read the small print.

Towards the end of my stint, a young girl, who was about 15-years-old, came to audition for Ambrose. She sang 'My

Yiddisher Mama' beautifully. Her name was Anne Shelton and one week later, SHE was doing the broadcasts and I was out of the picture. It was dawning on me that I was a member of a very tough profession, no longer child wonder 'Little Mary Lee', but just another jobbing dance band vocalist. It's a daunting transition, sliding from child star to adult status.

I truly started at the top and worked my way down. I remember being called into Leslie MacDonnell's office. He said he would only charge me 5% instead of the usual 10% of my earnings, but explained work would not be immediate as he was trying to establish me as an adult artist. I had never saved a penny in my life so, if I wanted to eat, I couldn't wait for the transition. I didn't sign with him, though it was probably the biggest mistake of my life. Had he offered me a retainer, I might have been a star all my life.

Instead, I signed for a year with another agent who could only offer me top of the bill spots in number 2 theatres. While it was not a good days' work when I signed with him, in a funny way, he pointed me to the Scottish scene, which has been my backbone ever since. I have never had to rely on London again, so some things in life are meant to be and there's a lot to be said for home.

The number 2 theatres were small and the pit orchestras that accompanied me were small, too.

The musical director was usually very intimidating and could play the run of the mill stuff, but when I put in front of him or his fellow musicians a really beautiful arrangement which had cost me a fortune to have written out, the usual remark was, 'What's this bloody rubbish?' covering up the fact that they couldn't read the difficult parts.

At first I just laughed and got through it somehow, but I found something in me was lost forever, the realisation that all musicians weren't top class, when I had known no other. So I compromised, and when you do that, you settle for second best and your artistry suffers. But if you need the money, you just have to get on with it.

The truth is that my act wasn't good enough. I wasn't singing commercial songs, just stringing a few numbers together and hoping for the best. I quickly learned to compromise, construct an act and sing numbers people instantly knew. It was commercial, but never really my cup of tea, and gave me no joy.

One of the shows I did at that time was 'Youth Swings Along'. I met and dressed with a nice young woman called Master Joe Peterson. She dressed like a choirboy and had some lovely recordings to her credit. Not long ago, they were brought out on compact disc. Her great artistry has stood the test of time, though she is no longer with us.

I vividly remember the day the Second World War broke out. I was working in an established summer show with comedians Jimmy Jewel and Ben Warris, at Torquay. I spent a lovely day basking in the sunshine, but on going to the theatre that night, was told the show was finishing . . . as all the shows did at the beginning of the war. People didn't really think war would break out. But, of course, it did, and from that moment onwards our lives were changed forever.

Two weeks later I packed up and boarded a train to London, to catch the express for Glasgow, and I was convinced I was going to be blown to bits on my way home! I still remember Euston Station, already awash with soldiers. I'd never seen a soldier before and was frightened they were going to shoot me on sight, quite forgetting they were on our side. I spent most of my journey home hiding in the loo. The door was battered with amazing regularity but I ignored their pleas.

I arrived in Glasgow with my luggage and my bag of furs. Furs were the 'in thing'. They were my pride and joy and I wasn't going to throw them out. My mum was pleased to see me and gave me her best bedroom, with the pink satin quilt. I felt secure and happy, but not for long.

The war was on, Germany had invaded Poland, but nobody had invaded Talla Road, Hillington and I was nostalgic for London. By now all my chums were there so I decided to pack up and go back to the life I knew best.

I thought the war would never knock on our door and it didn't for the best part of a year. The theatre had come into its own to help raise the nation's spirits, so work was plentiful. I'd had enough of the number 2 theatre circuit and went back to freelancing with bands again.

There was lots of broadcasting work, most of it done from the BBC studios in Bristol. I wasn't earning a fortune, but I was glad to be back with great musicians. I recall one particularly happy week appearing with the Squadronnaires, a London RAF band working with the Forces.

I lived in the Theatre Girls Club in Soho, which was cheap and cheerful. Run by the actress Fay Compton's mother, it was for girls looking for work, or training to teach ballet and tap and so on.

Sadly, when they found out I was working in night clubs around Soho, I was politely asked to leave to make way for a girl who needed the accommodation more than I did. I was sorry to go because it was the happiest of places to live, though the club was run on very strict lines. In the morning there were prayers, you queued up for lunch, and we slept in little communal 'dookets' with a screen across. A small wardrobe and a dresser were our furniture, but oh, the company was a hoot. We laughed until we cried.

We borrowed each others clothes if we were going for a night on the town, and if you wanted a late pass (out after 11pm) you had to ask the matron. Working in night clubs meant that I needed a pass every night, so they quickly rumbled me.

As we sang our nightly hymn before supper we could look out of the window and see the ladies of the night parading. They would make rude gestures to us, which I'll leave to your imagination! Matron would urge us not to look at them, but of course we took a damn good look, and knew most of them by name. They seemed nice girls to me, always beautifully turned out.

I look back on my days at the Theatre Girls Club with great affection.

At this point an agent advised me to take a summer season at the Cosy Corner in Dunoon, in Scotland. The atmosphere in London was not the best as the war was hotting up, so at least the move would reunite me with my parents and get me away from wartime London.

I was easily persuaded.

I was 19 and thought I knew 'where the monkey slept', show business wise, but nothing had prepared me for that Cosy Corner summer season. I thought it would be a breeze, sing a few songs, pick up my pennies and get a tan. My mother had taken a nice little bungalow in Dunoon to be with me and see to my creature comforts. That was the good part.

My name was like a beacon on the playbill, 'Mary Lee, Scotland's Own – direct from London's West End', but I knew hee-haw about the rigours involved in a Scottish summer season. I was soon to learn.

I arrived with three dresses and twelve orchestrations, which I thought would be more than enough. Wrong! What my London agent had omitted to tell me was that we would have to change the entire show twice weekly for twelve weeks, so twenty-four acts were needed. I went to my mother after a few days and announced my decision to 'jack it in', to which she replied, 'Oh no you're not, my lady. I've paid for this house for three months, and that's that.' I was indeed caught in the tender trap.

I had to do two singing spots per week, join the opening chorus, do sketches, dance, everything but make the tea. Could I cope? I had to, though it was a hard lesson.

The cast knew by my billing that I was earning more than them and gave me a hard time, but in a roundabout way it taught me a lot.

At the end of the season I could take on that type of show with the best of them. I was now Mary Lee, forgotten in England but doing away fine in Scotland.

And the war was on, so it seemed better for me to stay back home.

7

MARY'S WAR YEARS

When my London contract ended, I was being booked by William R. Galt, who resembled a Scottish Howard Hughes, a very reclusive man only seen, I suspect, by his immediate family. The agency was run by the legendary and very astute Nellie Sutherland, who was always kind and helpful and never bore a grudge. In those days, Mary Lee had a fiery temper and often walked out of shows on the Friday, only to be reinstated by the forgiving Nellie on the Monday to start another show.

She knew my worth and as long as I could produce the goods, I was in. At this time, a love of comedy entered my life. Nellie offered me a summer season at the Pavilion Theatre, Glasgow with the late Tommy Morgan, king of the Pavilion. It was an honour to be invited to join his summer show, which ran for six months – and the money was excellent.

It was wartime and the blackouts were strictly enforced. At the end of the second house I would grab my torch and run for the number 15 bus to Hillington. I had no fear of walking in the blackouts, only a fear of what might drop on me one fine night!

What a joy the Morgan show was, beautifully dressed and produced, and the Glasgow public was so kind to me in my new guise. Tommy used me in sketches, usually as the posh daughter. 'Mother, is my mince and totties ready?' I was a good foil for his rough humour. He also gave me a double act to do with him, which I loved. I used to get laughs where they weren't meant, but this magical big man never rebuked me. So I ad-libbed in the knowledge that it would always be received kindly.

Tommy Morgan was always magnificently dressed, loved a flutter and had a smashing car and chauffeur. He really enjoyed standing at the stage door waiting to see the punters going in to his show. Once inside, dressed and looked after by his faithful Mima and Arthur, he became the big, gallus case the public loved.

He loved to invite his cast to his flat for supper and always played Noel Coward numbers to entertain us. These happy evenings were spent in the block of flats I now live in, but in those days, an invitation to his flat was climbing the heights indeed.

During that time I was up to all my tricks. There was no shortage of good-looking men in the show and usually I didn't have any bother 'clicking' them. I'll let you into my secret. If they didn't succumb quickly enough, I fainted at their feet. It was my secret weapon, and I had it down to a fine art.

I'd hear them say, 'Mary has fainted, get a brandy.' Then a taxi would be called, with my poor victim in it with me. After that, the hook was nicely pulled in and another good man bit the dust!

But as far as men were concerned, I was all talk and no do. I was frightened of my father's wrath. I was worldly, but there were no partners, one night stands or anything of today's parlance. A wee snog in the back seat of a taxi did me nicely, thank you. But I was only 20 and, war or no war, life was for living.

We danced the night away in the Locarno Club or the Playhouse Ballroom, especially when Joe Loss and his orchestra came to Glasgow. I never hit the hay till 3am. No wonder my mother couldn't budge me in the mornings.

The wartime clothes were not unlike today's fashions. We wore stiletto heels and Betty Grable hairstyles. If you were flat-chested, you stuck in falsies and cheated. What the Lord has forgotten, let us pad with cotton.

At the end of the Morgan show, a bill-topping act came to the Empire Theatre called 'Stars of the Air' (no prizes for guessing television wasn't in full sway). The act included Maudie Edwards, vocalist Sam Browne, and ex-Ambrose drummer Max Bacon. I heard through the grapevine that Maudie was leaving, so I chanced my arm.

I wrote an act, learned it, and went up to the Central Hotel, where Sam and Max heard it and offered me the job. I joined the act at the Shepherd's Bush Empire in London. I loved being in it. The gowns were beautiful and making my entrance between two magnificent pianos did my ego a power of good.

The agent for 'Stars of the Air' was Joe Collins, father of Joan and Jackie, so that's where the girls get their business acumen. After six months the act broke up, so it was back to the 'buroo' again. I had filled a vacuum in a well-established act, and when that was finished, so was I.

I couldn't get work in London so I telephoned the stalwart Nellie Sutherland in Glasgow and she promptly booked me for my second summer season with Tommy Morgan. I knew the routine now, and the show was a labour of love.

As the season drew to a close, Tommy Morgan offered me Principal Girl in his forthcoming winter season at the Metropole Theatre in Glasgow. I said, 'No thank you, Mr. Morgan. I've only ever played the Empire or the Pavilion.' In my eyes, the Metropole was third class – I had a big head, indeed.

Mr. Morgan didn't take my refusal lightly. 'Well lassie,' he said, 'if it's good enough for me, it's good enough for you.' He was earning a fortune at the Metropole.

So, at the end of the season, we parted as friends, but never again were we workmates.

Years later, Mr. and Mrs. Alex Frutin, the owners of the Metropole Theatre, were to become my next door neighbours. He was a great character, but an early riser who used to ring my back door bell at 7am shouting, 'Open up and get the tea on.' The bell was removed and he would say, 'You need to get that bell fixed.' I was fond of Alex and Lily.

In the end, I didn't do a pantomime that year because I was called up. I duly presented myself to the Recruitment Officer, determined to convince him I would be of the utmost use in ENSA helping to entertain the troops and he did indeed enlist me for ENSA. You had to do six weeks a year entertaining the troops, wherever they decided to send you. I came away from the interview feeling very relieved, because it meant that I could continue my stage work and still do my bit for the war effort.

ENSA sent me to Catterick Camp in England. If you haven't sung with an army band, you haven't lived. I picked the right number, 'Strike Up the Band' and dressed in a red midi-coat and white pleated skirt. The band were similarly attired, with trousers instead of a skirt, of course, and we had a ball for the week.

But working for ENSA wasn't all beer and skittles. We were sent to an RAF base on the south coast, near Dover, with 16 rows of young fliers in the front rows, and the usual RAF complement at the back. The show was going great guns, then the sirens sounded. This happened a lot, and before you could say 'Boo', the front 16 rows were empty. Before you knew it, you were playing to an empty house.

Then you could hear the eerie drone of the planes taking off. Some of the pilots were no more than 20 years old and that's when I knew we were fighting a battle. It shook you into the reality of things.

Between ENSA stints I went back to the Scottish theatre and one particular week, in mid-March 1941, I was playing the Victory Theatre in Paisley. I had booked seats for the second house for my mum and dad and the opening chorus for the second house was underway when the sirens sounded. The comic walked forward and announced, 'Ladies and gentlemen, the sirens have just went, good grammar teached here.'

The audience had the choice of staying put or going home. Most of them sat tight and we sang every song we knew. The audience and I wearied at about 4am.

This raid, we realised, was very different. The skies all around us were lit with fires and the bombing was incessant. This was the bombing of Clydebank and 1200 people were killed in the Clydebank Blitz. What a disaster, and it was Hell on earth for the Bankies. Very few houses were spared.

Towards morning it ceased. My mum, dad and I huddled together backstage, hoping God would be good and spare our wee house. He was. When we got home my wee brother Eddie, who had never gone into a shelter during an air raid, could not be found. He had been down Paisley Road way and a bomb fell as near as dammit. Someone gave him a shovel to dig for bodies beneath the rubble. He was first in the shelter after that!

He didn't discuss it. He didn't have to. Eddie later served in the Navy and was proud to do so.

The bombing continued the next night for hour upon hour and I'll never forget those two nights. It was a bit of our history we could fine have done without.

During the war I started to take comedy seriously. I still loved singing, but knew I would always make a good living from comedy. I spent most of the 1940s perfecting the art and also writing scripts.

Nellie Sutherland sent me to the Gaiety Theatre in Ayr, to take the place of a lady who was going to America to join her husband, a squadron leader in the American Air Force. I was to do my singing act and appear with Dave Willis in sketches. When I arrived, Dave called me into his room and said, 'Miss Lee, welcome to the show. Pen and paper please. Write these gags down.' Then he said, 'And you will not say another word.'

I think someone had marked his cards that I had the habit of slipping in a couple of my own. Looking back, I don't blame him, but he never got the fun out of me that dear Tommy Morgan had.

I loved watching comics and was once on a variety bill with Will Fyfe. He had his dresser side stage, with a little tray to accommodate his different false teeth for his character parts. This fascinated me and each night I'd go to the side of the stage to watch his act.

One night, there was a knock at my dressing room door and Will's dresser said, 'Miss Lee, will you stop watching Mr. Fyfe every night. It's putting him off.' That was my gas in a peep.

I also met Sir Harry Lauder during the Morgan show. He was just an old man in a kilt to me. But I remember he said, 'You have a nice wee personality, lassie. Aye, and you'll go far.'

8

THE MIDDLE EAST

One day I had a telephone call from Harry Roy, a well known band leader of the day, inviting me to go to the Middle East with him to entertain the troops. I reported to Drury Lane in London to get my shots, then jumped on a train for Brighton to stay with friends. When I arrived, I couldn't lift my suitcase down from the luggage rack. My arm was swollen up like a balloon. Talk about suffering for your art.

Harry Roy had three girl singers, me, Marjorie Kingsley, and a lovely girl called Myra, whose surname escapes me now. We took a train from London to Southampton, and boarded the troopship SS *Stratheden*. The sleeping arrangements were hilarious, with 100 WAAFs, 100 WRENs, 100 ATS and 100 ENSA aboard. We slept in hammocks, 100 to a room. I had a pal in the Navy and he advised me to wear a money belt with anything I valued in it. This I did.

He also said, 'If you're pipped,' meaning if the ship goes down, 'don't go where you're told to go. In an emergency, find your own way up to the deck.' We had boat drill every day, and it certainly wasn't 'ladies first'. The majority would have stood on your head to make a quick getaway. I prayed it would never be for real. But it was close. The ship in front of us was 'pipped', but all survived, though they arrived in Egypt with only what they were standing up in. So we were lucky.

We dined with the officers and I always kept my fresh fruit for the tommies. They liked that. We did three performances on the way out, all well received.

The ship was 'dry' – no drinking – and I filled in the dull evenings after dinner reading the cards. I'd choose an officer who was well-read and educated, and he'd fall for it like a ton of bricks. I don't regret a minute of it. If I was skint today, I'd take a booth in Blackpool and do it again. I pretended to read the cards – I had the gift of the gab and a vivid imagination but I'd never done it before that voyage!

We docked at Port Said, and went on by train to Cairo. It was a sight to behold in every way. The locals standing on the banks of the Nile used to wave something at us, and it wasn't their hanky! That's when I learned a good yard stick. We screamed with laughter. We were on a moving train so it wasn't a problem, but it did keep us amused.

On our arrival in Cairo we were billeted at the famous Shepherds Hotel, three girls to a room. On our first morning, going into the bathroom, I saw a battery of ants marching across the floor. You could never shift them, just batter them into submission until the next batch arrived. We had a couple of days before the start of the tour so we set off to discover Cairo. It was magnificent, with lovely sunshine, white houses and colourful cars. To me it was complete Paradise.

Our six week tour consisted of going up and down the line, the line being Egypt, Jerusalem and Beirut, and we did our first show in Ismailia.

I remember that well, because I had a tooth pulled out by an Army dentist there. I had never felt pain like it and remember thinking, 'God help the troops.' We visited the Wailing Wall in Jerusalem and I loved Beirut, such a modern pulse, even all those years ago. We performed each night to those who were able to come to the show, but my greatest joy was to go round the wards accompanied by a young officer who introduced me to the lads, especially the 'jocks'. I'd say, 'What would you like me to sing?' then I'd just belt it out unaccompanied.

One night a young lad got his fiddle out and played 'Danny Boy'. I sang it. A nurse said, 'That was nice Mary. That wee chap is very ill.' It would have broken your heart.

I liked being with the Harry Roy band. They were a cheery crowd. Up to this point in my life I was a confident woman, able to take whatever came my way. But the Middle East was to be my bête noir. I had never had a nerve in my body and now, suddenly, I developed a fear of performing. This fear got steadily worse with each performance. Perspiration lashed down my hands. My heart pounded. I had an awful wish to turn around and run like hell the other way. One night, I ran on to do my act and the audience swam around me.

Down I went, flat on the stage.

A young Army doctor was called and I was taken back to the hotel and given a sedative. The band went on to their next destination. What else could they do? The young doctor was my lifeline. I would beg him to let me come on his rounds. I only felt like the old Mary when I was with him. For some reason the fear disappeared in his presence. But the officer in charge of entertainment had me brought back to Cairo, and hospitalised there.

The band finished their tour of duty, visited me in hospital, and left for home and family. I had no visible sign of illness, just this terrible fear of performing, and shattered nerves. It was a good old-fashioned breakdown, of course, but nobody told me what was wrong. All I knew was I felt safe in the hospital.

When I was released from hospital about a month later, I walked out by myself and got a taxi to my hotel. ENSA offered me two choices. I could go around the smaller bases with a little company or go home. I plumped for the first.

The tour was to last three weeks. Then my nerves started playing me up again. I desperately wanted to go home. This was pre Valium and antidepressant days. They were non-existent in my recovery. A breakdown then was very misunderstood. It was up to yourself and the stock phrase was 'Pull yourself together.'

Eventually I packed it in and boarded a boat in Port Said, to take me out to a troop ship. Or so I thought. It stopped at a slightly bigger ship, and we embarked. This ship had come from the Far East, bringing home sick cases from that part of the world.

The ENSA complement included the actor Ralph Michael, who at that time was married to the actress Fay Compton. As we had little to do in the evenings during the voyage home, we decided to do a show for the crew. We had no musicians, no nothing, so we announced the acts by ringing the ships' bell to bring us on. To finish the show, Ralph Michael did a touching speech from Noel Coward's 'Cavalcade'. There wasn't a dry eye in the house.

Eventually I arrived home to Isa and Willie and wartime Britain. Me with my beautiful Cairo leather luggage set, which fell to pieces after the first shower of rain!

My poor mother didn't know how to help me. If I saw any of my pals in the street, I'd go to the other side of the road to avoid them – not like me at all. She was kind, but wished I'd get out of the house and get a job.

I used to go for walks by myself and cry all the way, there and back. I longed for sympathy but got none, because they just thought I was a pain in the neck . . . and I was.

One morning, whilst having my morning bout of crying, I suddenly realised there was only one person who could help me. Myself. So I telephoned Nellie Sutherland at the Galt Agency. Nellie, not knowing my troubles, asked if I had enjoyed the Middle East. I heard myself say, 'It was smashing, Nellie, but I'm free to work again.'

She, as always, said, 'You start at the Gaiety Theatre in Leith on Monday.'

It was the hardest telephone call I have ever made. But it was to be my strength for the rest of my days. From then on, I swore I would show myself I could get back to square one. It was not easy, but I did it.

It didn't happen overnight. I still had the constant fear before I went on, but as the weeks went by, it was getting easier for me. Maybe I'd go for four nights with no nerves, thoroughly enjoying the show, then it would hit me again. But by now I knew how to deal with my fears. By confronting them, I grew stronger in every way. So much so, if anyone was off the show and someone had to stand in for them, the producers would say, 'Ask Mary, she'll do it.' I taught myself to have the toughest nerves in show business. It was my hardest task, but so worthwhile.

The faithful Nellie Sutherland then sent me over to the Empire Theatre in Belfast, to play Principal Boy in 'Aladdin'. I loved playing Principal Boy. It gave scope for my youthful acting talent, learned at my mother's long mirror. The Empire was a fine little theatre, beautifully run, with shows produced by Pat McKay. I made my entrance as the boy Aladdin and the Belfast audience gave me a nice welcome. I bowed and mouthed 'Thank you', before starting my opening speech.

When I finished the scene, Pat McKay said, 'Mary, never acknowledge a round of applause in a panto or a play.' Lesson learned.

It was great training throwing your voice to the back of the gallery. We had centre microphones, but not the delightful clip on version used in today's pantomimes. Each night I was put into the cave by the baddie, and one night a wee voice shouted, 'Let that woman out of the cave!'

We had great fun, and it was a joy to do.

I had to dye my hair black for that show. It was pre-wig days

South Africa, to save being caught by the German U boats.' It was a long way for a short cut.

The Regiment went on to Cape Town and eventually to the Suez Canal, right through the Middle East as far as Damascus, then returned to Egypt and boarded a train to Port Said.

'Ah good,' Jack thought, 'we're going home.'

Not so. They were headed for India and it was a four day train journey to Calcutta. From there they made their way to Imphal on the Burmese border where they were stationed in huts in the jungle.

Most of the boys had never travelled anywhere more exotic than Largs and it was an incredible experience for them as well as a bit of a culture shock. Jack told me this amazing story.

'One night, Mary, I was coming back from the canteen and I started to cry. For no reason at all, tears were dropping out of my eyes. I couldn't understand it, and eventually made my way back to my hut.'

Well, about a fortnight later, Jack got a letter from his mother, telling him his father had died from a heart attack.

When he looked at the date on the letter, Jack realised that his father had died the very night he had walked about the jungle crying! It was obvious to him then that he had experienced a premonition that something was very wrong at home.

Jack was always curious, and a bit of a rebel against authority, character traits that caused him to very nearly lose his life while the regiment was in Imphal. Expressly against orders, he wandered into a neighbouring village and was looking around when he heard the drone of a flight of aeroplanes in the distance, and assumed they were British bombers. Fortunately, they were flying so low that as they came closer he could see the pilots, and my God, they were Japanese! He got the fright of his life and dived headfirst into the gutter at the side of the road which was full of muck and rubbish. He ended up in a hell of a mess . . . but it probably saved his life!

It was an example of his quick reactions in dangerous circumstances – brought about by his own actions perhaps – but nonetheless, his nerve saved the day. No wonder facing tough theatre audiences held no fears later on, in his life in show business.

In due course, the Regiment left the Burmese border and Jimmy Cruden was ready for his first taste of performing to a large audience. He was sent to Calcutta to do a big charity show for the troops. He did gags about the Army and finished with a tap dance in his kilt, with his army boots on. It was a big success, and he had a great write-up in a newspaper published for the Forces in Calcutta called 'Beezer' (British Entertainment Services). The review said that Jack had the timing of Max Wall and the personality of Bob Hope, and that he would go as far as either of them. The reviewer was Ross Parker, the man who wrote the immortal song 'There'll Always Be An England'. Not bad for a beginner and from then on, Jack knew he wanted to perform.

Jack also learned to love Indian food in the Army. The British troops were served up soya bean 'meat' and other bland, tasteless food, so Jack would cross over to the Indian line to get his ration of curry, rice and maybe a chapati.

His pals would say, in the rather crude terms used at that time, 'There's the wog away over for his dinner,' but Jack paid no heed. He was the one eating tasty grub, after all! Many years on, when we had settled down together and went to visit his mother, she would say, 'Are you going out to one of those Indian shops again? You'd be far better making him mince and tatties at home.' It was all very different in those days in Scotland. You ate fish and chips and pie and beans and there weren't the Chinese, Indian and other rich and varied cuisines we take for granted nowadays.

Jack had a wonderful memory, and could recall highlights from his time in India and Burma that lived on with him forever. Earl Mountbatten had written to the appropriate authorities in London and said our troops out in Burma and India had no entertainment at all. They heard the occasional radio show, like Vera Lynn, but had no formal shows or the like.

Back came a reply saying that Noel Coward was being flown out to India on a special plane, complete with a white piano! The great man gave an open air show to all the Services personnel in Chittagong, near the Burmese border. Jack recalled sitting on the ground and watching Coward in inimitable action at his white piano.

Coward had taken the trouble to do his homework, and even re-wrote the lyrics to 'Let's Do It', putting in witty references to people in the regiment. All much appreciated by the homesick troops.

At this stage in the war the Americans were stationed near Imphal and from time to time Jack and his mates in the regiment were invited over to their camp. They laid on doughnuts and real coffee, hot dogs and steaks for their guests, and they were entertained by the cream of American talent, like Mickey Rooney. Years later, we both met Rooney when he came to Glasgow to do his one man show at the King's Theatre. Funny, isn't it, how life can come full circle sometimes.

Jack arrived back in Britain after a mercifully uneventful five year stint, but the army was not finished with him yet.

The Black Watch, or at least Jacks' regiment, was sent to Norway as the Army of Occupation, so after SIX years' service he was demobbed, in 1946. Each man was kitted out for civilian life, given a suit, a trilby hat, a pair of gloves, shoes, a shirt and a tie, all in a cardboard box. And along with their demob suit, everybody was given leave pay of about £150. All the 'spivs', the wide boys, would be waiting at the barracks gates. And when Jack was offered £5 for his cardboard box, he gladly sold it . . . I ask you! Mind you, the spivs did a roaring trade, and a fiver was a lot of money then.

During his time in the Forces, Jack had arranged for two shillings a week to be paid to his mother from his army pay and, when he was demobbed, she handed him £60. She had saved up every penny to give him on his return. In today's money, I'd guess it would be worth over £1,000. Jack never forgot that.

When we'd talk about how we started out in showbiz Jack would always say to me, 'I wasn't lucky like you, Mary. I had it really tough to begin with in show business.' And I suppose he was right.

His first appearance after his army days was at the Queen's Theatre in Glasgow, known for its very tough audiences. And that night, they were running true to form, very restive, and had thrown pennies at the act on before him, but Jack just picked them up and said, 'Thanks. That'll do me for my fare home.' They warmed to him right away.

Jack appeared on stage in his army kilt, with taps on his army boots and I think this also made quite an impression. He went on to do three pantomimes at the Queen's Theatre, just dipping his toes in the stormy waters of variety at the time.

Shortly before our fateful meeting in Belfast, the famous Nellie Sutherland of the Galt Theatrical Agency in Glasgow sent Jack down to London to make a film with Max Bygraves and Hal Monty, called 'Bless 'Em All.'

Hal Monty played the comic character, Max was the love interest – the young lad who had all the girls falling for him – and Jack was the archetypal Scottish soldier. An army picture, it was produced by Arthur Dent, who could make a full length comedy feature in under three weeks. They couldn't believe it in Wardour Street! Jack said it was because Arthur always used the first take of each scene, even if the director wanted to do it again.

Jack just fell into filming. He loved it, and said the only aspect he hated was the discipline of having to present yourself at 6am at the Bushey Film Studios for make up. Like me, he wasn't good at early starts. The film was a success, and Jack savoured seeing his name in lights for the very first time at a cinema in London's Petticoat Lane.

Max Bygraves went on from there to do a radio programme called 'Educating Archie' with Archie Andrews, which made him famous. Jack Milroy headed back up north to a theatre job in Belfast and a date with destiny.

10

ENTER JACK

I remember clearly I was in the stalls during rehearsals with my fellow performers when I spotted this fellow walking down the flight of wooden stairs which took you to stage level. He was wearing a kilt that poked out four inches below his navy raincoat and his legs were so thin I thought he had tossed a sparrow and lost. But when I saw the face, I tell you, he was easily the most handsome man I'd ever set eyes on. And the nicest thing about him was that he was quite unaware of the impact he had on the opposite sex.

I was soon to get to know him, and realised the only thing he was interested in was show business, and all the watering holes in Belfast. He wasn't a big drinker, he just liked the odd beer, but he loved the company.

Jack joined the Spring Show the following Monday and he partnered me in the opening snow scene. We came down in pairs, to the strains of 'Winter Wonderland'. There was a lovely round of applause, and, out of the corner of my mouth, I whispered, 'It's not for you.'

And it wasn't, because they didn't know him, but they certainly knew me.

Jack told me years later that before my remark he had been really chuffed and couldn't believe his warm reception, but after it he thought, 'This is a right cheeky bugger I've got hold of here.

'Imagine saying that on an opening night,' he said, 'When I was up to high doh with nerves!'

We didn't do a double act the first week. I used that to size up his work. I stood at the side of the stage as he did his 'classy' act – blazer, white slacks, white shirt and shoes. He sang a song, did some patter and the same finish as he always did, two choruses of 'Suzie' and a tap dance. He was nicely received but if he was going to do double acts with Mary he had to rethink his clothes, his approach to comedy and get the attention away from that beautiful face.

Come to think of it, with the right material Jack would have made a good modern stand-up comic. He always had that wonderful, infectious laugh – a gift for a comic.

When he finished his act, I was there, bold as brass. My first words were, 'Oh son, it won't do. You'll need to roughen up your comedy.'

In those days you had to be visually funny, so I said so.

'I'll give you a double act script,' I said. 'Take it home and we'll rehearse it tomorrow morning.'

I knew where all the laughs lay, and if he changed his clothes and funnied up his face, we were home and dry. We did our first double the next week, a comedy soprano and tenor, and Jack took to it like a duck to water. Don't forget, I had to do likewise, funny face, hair scraped back, two cushions with string around the waist to enhance my 'derriere', so it was horses for courses. During the act, neither of us was much to look at, but we had the common joy of looking for laughs, and getting them.

It was purely business. I enjoyed his company and it was to be many a long day before we looked at each other in a different light. Jack had travelled the world with the Army and was just getting the chance to sow his wild oats, and who could blame him?

When we finished the season, Jack had come on by leaps

and bounds and was loved by the Belfast people. We went our separate ways which was the way it happened then. You could work with a person and then perhaps not see them for a year or so, depending on where you were playing.

At the end of the show, I got a call from Nellie Sutherland telling me that Jack Milroy was to be the principal comic at the Tivoli Theatre in Aberdeen the following summer. Would I like to join him as his comedy woman? Was it fate that I was to rejoin he of the beautiful face? Was it hell. He knew I had all these double acts up my sleeve, could write sketches and that I'd be a big help to him. And it was all fine by me.

So there we were again, Milroy and Lee. The show was presented by William Cummings, a modest and kindly man, and it was to be a hard working season. We opened in May and ran until October. Six months, and they couldn't get enough of us.

Jack had all the ideas for sketches, and brilliant they were, too. I then had to burn the midnight oil to have the script ready to hand out to the company but Jack was a joy to write for. What I wrote, and what was actually performed were two subtlely different things. Once Jack worked the material, put his own comedy stamp on, it was his forever and it was brilliant.

The show was called 'Whirl of Laughter' and Jack broke all existing records for the Tivoli. We did two shows a night, and the second house queue was waiting from 7pm each night for the 8.30pm show.

Jack was beginning to taste success. He still wasn't earning a great deal of money, but like myself in the old days, he was learning his craft. He didn't start at the top and work his way down, as I did. Jack gradually worked his way up, which, of course, is the best way.

William Cummings took us down to London to tour our 'Whirl of Laughter' but I wouldn't say we whirled. It was more like a gentle flutter. But it did teach Jack and I that our comedy was for Scotland.

When it finished, I joined a touring English show. Alex Munro – the father of Janet Munro the film star – was the comic. During our week in Aldershot, I got a call from Jack Milroy saying he was coming down to see me.

'Things are looking up,' I thought to myself.

Typically, he came by bus. He was Capricorn and not exactly the last of the big spenders. When he arrived his back was causing him agony, so it was off to the Turkish baths for him.

Now, if I'm honest, we had slowly become quite fond of one another but I did have serious reservations at the back of my mind. I really wanted a 'nine to five' man, and to live the simple life. I was tired of touring and wanted to settle in a place of my own so the prospect of hooking up with someone else from the business wasn't all that appealing, no matter how handsome he was.

The charming Mr. Cummings booked us for the next summer season, which was 1952, at the Tivoli Theatre in Aberdeen, and during it the irresistible force overcame the immovable object and the inevitable happened.

Jack and I got married!

11

OUR NUPTIALS
AND THE START OF THE WHIRL

We were married at three o'clock in the afternoon and back on the stage at the Tivoli Theatre in Aberdeen for the first house. Yes, we even did two shows at night on the day we had the ceremony. All the punters shouted, 'Hard up'.

It was a comedy wedding, right down to Jack's tartan bunnet. My daddy came up to the wedding but not my mother. She loved Jack, but hated leaving the house. She was agoraphobic before we even knew what the condition was.

Jack's mother came up and shared a room with me prior to the wedding. She nearly blew me out of the room with her snoring and I went to the wedding like a washed out rag. The wedding photographs show a caring, loving Jack, and an exhausted looking Mary. It was the first and last time I shared a room with Jack's mother Mary.

Cliff Jordan, the band leader at the Tivoli, owned a hotel in town, and gave us a room for nothing for a couple of nights. The wedding tea was an 'all you could eat for a shilling' do, but at least my parents were spared all the palaver of today's weddings, costing thousands of pounds. All ours cost was a ring, the licence and a new outfit.

After our couple of nights of luxury, we went back to our

digs till the show finished. We stayed with a wee gem in Aberdeen, an unclaimed treasure called Nanny Martin. She ran the best digs in Aberdeen, as well the funniest and the kindest. She had a large four poster bed in her 'best' letting room, and she laughed heartily as she told us she once had the seven dwarfs from 'Snow White' sleeping in it. She described them as dreeping down from the four poster onto a lemonade box, and then on to the floor.

'Oh, Mary,' she said. 'They were dirty wee men. They kept feeling my leg!'

She'd float into the room with a bundle of sausages on a plate and talk about 'Sodgers' cockies, Mary,' and roar with laughter. Being in her company was a lift to the soul. All the pros stayed there, in the Penthouse, as she called it, a slanty room with four beds in it.

Scotland's king of country music, Sydney Devine, was one of her favourite boys, and I'm sure he thought the world of wee Nanny. She had been a landlady all her life, and her mother before her, and she looked after Jack and I like a clucking hen.

We loved playing jokes on her. She'd often give us stew and dough balls for our supper and the dough balls were fine as long as you weren't crossing on the ferry. When she left the room, Jack and I would fling them on the fire, and when she returned she'd say, 'My, that fire's fairly blazing up.' Little did she know!

Years later, Jack and I were doing a television show from Aberdeen and we told the story about Nanny's dough balls. The next day we took a trip up to see her and she was dancing up and down with joy.

'Oh Mary,' she said, 'I've been out for my messages and everyone's stopped me. I feel like a star.' Well, in our minds, she was always a star.

One other odd thing about Nanny's house was the loo. It

was a fair old size and against one wall there was a wardrobe and a sewing machine. The running gag was that Nanny had a beautifully furnished loo and her smallest room was always a talking point for performers who stayed there. She was eccentric, and the world is a poorer place without her like.

Our experiences on the last nights of an Aberdeen show certainly proved that the tale about Aberdonians being mean is a fallacy. It would take the usherettes about an hour to bring the presents up on stage. You could have furnished your house with the gifts given to us, everything from a dinner set to a bundle of yellow fish. What lovely people, the salt of the earth. To this day I am still stopped by people saying, 'Mary, I was one of the crowd at your wedding.'

We spent our honeymoon in London, in a nice Italian hotel/restaurant called Ollivelli's, just off Tottenham Court Road. It was a popular place for showbiz people – they all went there for Mamma Ollivelli's suppers. Jack and I arrived after a long train journey. It wasn't your five hour trip in those days and I was jiggered after the journey and said to Jack, 'I think I'll have a wee sleep.' The bold Jack happily left me to take a bus 'up West' to see what shows were on. This was around 2pm and when I woke up later on the room was bitterly cold and there was no sign of Jack.

There was still no Jack at 8.30pm. He finally arrived back bearing flowers, which he got right over his napper, along with a few little gems flung in like 'fine honeymoon this is, I'd be better in a home with my hair cut!'

I soon calmed down, got dressed and we went to a welcoming English pub with a roaring coal fire. And after a couple of glasses of white wine, I saw him through different eyes. Always stage struck from his early Glasgow days of visits to the galleries for sixpence, I think he had collected every playbill in London. But he certainly selected the crème de la crème.

We went to see Valerie Hobson and Herbert Lom in 'The

King and I' at the London Palladium, and afterwards at Ollivelli's, who was at the next table? Herbert Lom. Great excitement, indeed.

When I got to back to our room I picked up my pen and paper and wrote a letter to Miss Hobson telling her how much I had enjoyed her performance. By return of post I received a beautiful, hand-written letter of thanks, saying how much she appreciated my letter, especially as I was also a member of the showbiz profession. That taught me a lesson. Always answer your fan mail promptly, and with gratitude. She was a lovely, well-bred and talented lady.

Jack and I used to agree to disagree about matinee days in London. Jack loved to visit Mr. William Hill in Soho – I loved straight plays. I'd go alone, but always found a kindred spirit to chat to in the audience. I loved the legit. theatre' because I had no knowledge of the workings of it. In Variety I knew every trick, even to singing a song while thinking what I would have for supper that night. But it wasn't for Jack. He loved musical comedy and seeing a stage brim full with people, just like his father did. Before their weekly departure to the galleries his dad would always ask Jack, 'How many on the stage tonight, lad?' If the answer was 'Forty, Father,' then they were both in Heaven. We had a marvellous fortnight, taking in all the shows and looking for Chinese restaurants which were few and far between in those days.

The happy honeymooners arrived home to play the Victory Theatre in Paisley . . . back to 'auld clothes and porridge' as they say in the best of circles. For the first time, we met a good looking young man who came from Paignton, and was to become Jack's comedy 'feed' and right hand man for the best part of the next ten years. It was Glen Michael, later to find his own fame with Scottish Television's 'Cartoon Cavalcade' series for children.

Jack was indeed lucky, because Glen was the best feed in

the business, and an excellent character actor, to boot. We three worked happily together for the next few years as Jack slowly but surely climbed the ladder to fame. There were fifty-two weeks' work in the year, if you wished to play it, and all the training in the world, sadly lost to today's generation. If today's performers could follow the sort of apprenticeship that Jack had it would be so good for them. By that I mean the amateur theatre where Jack first trod the boards as a lad. It's a great training ground.

Back to Milroy and Lee. Yes, it was Milroy and Lee, and you'd have needed a spy glass to see my billing in the 1950s and 60s, but it was no trauma to me. There were two pay packets coming into the same house and I was laughing all the way to the bank.

In 1953 Jack was approached by Eric Popplewell, owner of the Gaiety Theatre in Ayr. Eric was a nice man, and unknown to us, had been watching Jack and Glen working together for a couple of years. He was very particular that his comics should have material suitable for a family audience seaside show and after seeing us working at the Aberdeen Tivoli, Eric finally decided Jack was ready to come to Ayr. Jack was thrilled when the call came.

Eric always called Jack 'Jeek', and if rehearsals ran late, would send us home in lovely taxis. The resident show always went on tour, first stop Aberdeen, and Eric would have us all on stage, warning us to look after our props, saying, 'We must keep clean for Aberdeen.' The theatre was his life and Jack had much to thank him for.

Jack first starred in a 'Gaiety Whirl' summer season in 1954. It ran for twenty-one weeks. Indeed, for many, it was Jack who put the post-war Whirl into the Gaiety, when he led the company for six summer seasons, followed in the 1960s by Johnny Beattie.

Jack had a very special reason to remember that first season.

I was fully occupied elsewhere, but HE had an impromptu party in the stalls' bar with the cast and the champagne flowed to celebrate our son Jim's arrival! Jack described it as 'a memorable season anyway, well and truly topped by the birth of my son.'

When Jim was a toddler, he spent time with us at the theatre, playing with the props backstage and using dressing room wardrobes as hidey-holes while we rehearsed the following week's show.

Every night at the Gaiety, you could spot the regulars. If you didn't have a booking you often had to queue for a seat, and sometimes the queue stretched right round the theatre and back to the stage door! One regular, a farmer's wife, was a godsend to starving pros. Every weekend she loaded her car boot with a dozen eggs for each member of the cast, plus home made scones, pancakes and bacon. We all came to rely on her for our Sunday breakfasts and when she didn't make it one week it was a catastrophe. Her name was Bessie Murdoch, and legend has it she came to the theatre every week for 25 years. She had a block booking on a Saturday night for her family and friends, and brought the same 'goodies' for each cast. They don't make fans like that any more.

At the end of the 1955 season at Ayr, we were taking a stroll along the promenade at the end of the run when the lady from the Gaiety office came rushing to find us. There was an urgent telephone call from Glasgow. Could we come and take Tommy Morgan's place at the opening of his summer show at the Glasgow Pavilion? Tommy had taken ill and was unable to kick off his opening night.

We were dying to go off on holiday but, as always, Nellie Sutherland was persuasive, and Jack was keen to do it. In his young days, of course, he loved going to the Pavilion, sitting up in the gallery. In the late 1930s you paid your sixpence and watched the great stars like Jack Anthony, Will Fyfe and Dave

Willis. The Pavilion had been Jack's great hunting ground, so it was an immense thrill for him to be asked to appear there.

The late, great Morgan used to play to capacity audiences every night during his summer seasons, in sumptuously staged shows. Back in those days the casts were large and the productions were lavishly dressed, something you rarely see nowadays because of the expense involved. Tommy always had twenty girls in his troupe, the Morganettes.

The show was a big box office draw, and Tommy was much loved by Glasgow. The Pavilion asked us to take over the comedy side of the show so we rushed to the theatre at 10 o'clock on the Monday morning, and rehearsed right through until 6.30pm, just before the first house. We learned a sketch, then did our own material. Jack and I did a double act, and Jack did a solo spot.

The opening came and the company sang the opening chorus. We were standing behind the curtain waiting for our entrance when a voice offstage announced that owing to illness, Tommy Morgan would not be appearing. There was a loud groan of dismay from the audience, of course. Then the voice went on 'but we are very fortunate to have secured the services of Jack Milroy and Mary Lee' and there was an even BIGGER groan from the audience! Nobody knew who we were – we had never appeared together in Glasgow before. It took until halfway through the show before they got to grips with our style of comedy but we struggled on and deputised for Tommy for three weeks. In the end, Jack was so badly paid he thought it wasn't worth the hassle, so we left them to get on with it.

We had, however, dipped our toes in the Glasgow water that was to embrace Jack wholeheartedly for the rest of his life. But it took maybe five more years to become established in Glasgow. Funny that, when you think about it, when we were both Glaswegians.

At that time, of course, you started out at the Ayr Gaiety, the jumping off place for all the great stars. Dave Willis, Jack Anthony and Lex McLean all started at the Gaiety, establishing their names, THEN they went on to Glasgow and the challenges of one of the biggest and toughest audiences there was. The Gaiety was the gateway to the big shows in Glasgow.

The year we hurriedly journeyed up to Glasgow from Ayr to take over was when Morgan began to be very ill indeed and he never appeared at the Pavilion again. So who could fill his shoes? A fellow called Lex McLean was doing well in Edinburgh at the time – an odd man, but a very great comic. He was approached to replace Morgan, and did very well.

Lex would do a summer season that ran for six months. Imagine that! Then we would take over for the pantomime season. Morgan and McLean were the two big draws, and when they both went they WERE irreplaceable, and that was when the Pavilion lost its summer seasons – there was nobody who could step into their shoes.

We carried on visiting the cities we had success in – Aberdeen, Ayr, Dundee and Edinburgh, with Jack continuing to perfect his trade all the while.

Everyone loved Jack. He was so likeable, and gave no grief.

By this time, our family had arrived, daughter Diana and son Jim. School, and everything about settling down, beckoned. And at long last I was to have a little place of my own.

I left show business at the end of a summer season in Dundee, and went home to 8, Hatton Gardens, Cardonald in Glasgow . . . and the good life.

12

HOME BITTERSWEET HOME

I had made it, got my lovely house, literally down the road from my mother. I left show business and settled down with Jack and our children in our first real home. At long last we were all together – Jack, Jim, Diana and me. I put such love into the décor of that house, little knowing that Jack had no interest whatsoever in houses, how they looked, or what made them tick. He just took it for granted, but of course he had his showbiz life to think about and when I was working with him it was all I ever thought about too. It is a business you have to give one hundred per cent of your time to, and everything else is just daily life, which utterly escapes you. Honestly, if I had painted the house black and silver, Jack would have looked out of the window and said, 'My, these hills are lovely.' He only saw what was outside.

He finished a season at Dundee and arrived for his first night at home in his new abode. The children were in bed and I had the full make up on, dressed in a pretty dress and wearing a frilly apron, the perfect little housewife awaiting him at the door. Instead of taking me in his arms and saying, 'Isn't this wonderful,' the bold Jack said, 'Get all these bloody lights out. This place looks like Dixons Blazes.' (Whatever that might mean.)

So my cards were marked from day one.

I have to say that the first few months of my settling down

period were the unhappiest of my life. I had really thought it would be 'happy families', but too much water had gone under the bridge for it to work out as I had imagined. First of all, from my point of view, I had been travelling since the age of fourteen and knew no other life. My meals had been made for me by good and bad landladies. I never had to do any housework and I really couldn't even boil an egg.

So picture the scene. At 7.30am the alarm went and I'd be up like a linnet for the school run. The routine was clean out the fire, put the sticks and coal in, light the fire, set the table then waken the kids and make breakfast. Diana had school meals so she was away till about 4.30pm. Jim was round my feet. There were no pre-school facilities in those days – you were on your own.

Jack would be wakened in time to get to his rehearsals at 10am at the theatre. For me it was housework and pushing Jim in his pram. Jack came home at 2pm for lunch and a little sleep, then off to work at the Pavilion or whatever theatre he was appearing in.

No rest for me, of course, with the kids' tea to prepare, homework, baths and bed, with Jim coming down the stairs for the fifth time saying, 'Can I have a drink of water?'

Jack would then be home for supper and I'd always ask, 'What happened tonight in the theatre, Jack?' And he'd trot out his standard reply, 'Oh, just the usual, Mary.'

To which I'd reply, 'Something must have happened.'

I wanted all the gossip that I missed so much but Jack was just too tired to be bothered. Then it was icy silence and then off to bed for MORE icy silence.

I was not a happy bunny. I missed all my pals in the theatre, all the laughs we had back stage. Funnily enough, I didn't miss the performing. I was glad to be finished with that, but I had no idea that my new life would be so utterly different from my showbiz existence.

God help him, Jack did his best, and it was my decision to leave show business. That wasn't the hard part, because the business is a tough game. I missed the closeness Jack and I had always had all our married and professional lives. We were in each others company twenty-four hours a day, not realizing how lucky we were to work and live together so happily.

But children change lives, and I really thought it would be blissful for us all – the fairy tale, if you like. I really got the rough end of the stick, though, because Jack's life went on as usual. He just got other feeds and comedy women to work with him and he soon got used to that. But it did pull us apart for quite a long time.

I began to resent him going off to work every night leaving me with the chores and child rearing. But please don't misunderstand me. I still loved the man with all my heart, and if he had shown me just a little more understanding of how tough my situation was I could have got to terms with my lot a bit quicker. But Jack was never demonstrative. He loved to be made a fuss of but somehow found it hard to be loving.

But he showed his affection in so many other ways. For example, he would finish a week at Aberdeen and jump in the car after the second show on the Saturday, drive through the night to get home, then leave at the crack of dawn on the Monday for the drive back to Aberdeen, in order to spend some time with us. He was the best father ever.

I recall him doing things like coming to be at our children's Christmas party between the matinee and the evening show, dressed as Santa Claus. When Jack went back to work, Jim said, 'You know, Santa was wearing the same shoes as my daddy.' The innocence of youth.

And Jack could also be a considerate husband. When I was first pregnant, he was a riot. He used to squeeze six oranges every morning and told me if I drank the juice it would keep me thin. (I wish.) At the end of the season, I was eight months pregnant and still working. Jack would say, 'I'll just keep you for the comedy, Mary,' and he dressed me in big, bulky army greatcoats and so forth, to hide my bump. It wasn't the done thing then to flaunt your pregnancy or 'flash the bump' like they do today.

Jack would say, 'Ach, Mary, the audience will never know.'

On the last night, the presents came up. I got twenty pairs of baby shoes for starters. You name it, I got it . . . so much for the orange juice!

And he could make unexpected gestures. One day, out of the blue, he said, 'Mary, if you can pass your driving test I'll buy you a nice wee car.' Can a duck swim? I'm not saying it was easy, but after three failures I passed my test and got my first car, a white Ford. I have enjoyed driving ever since.

Jack was such a hard worker, and a really good man. Like every other professional comic, he had to give his all to his work. Of course I should have known that, but I never felt really close to Jack for the next few years. He simply would not let me in, never discussed comedy sketches or what was going on in his theatrical life. Like many other performers, he was a very shy, introverted man off the stage but brilliant once he stepped on it.

Larry Marshall used to write sketches for him when he was performing at the Glasgow Pavilion and the Gaiety Theatre in Ayr and they would meet at Central Station for the hand over of the script. On one occasion, Larry said, 'I'll have to stop writing for you, Jack. I'm doing a new thing up at Scottish Television. I don't know what it's all about. It's called "The One O'Clock Gang".'

Larry found much fame in the show, which ran for years, the cast being Dorothy Paul, Charlie Sim, dear Moira Brody, the Irish singer/pianist, and Jimmy Nairn, father of Nick Nairn, the celebrated cook.

Another fine writer, Stan Mars, did scripts for Jack in those early years and Stan also invented Francie and Josie, in a sketch he wrote for Rikki Fulton and Stanley Baxter – later to became Milroy and Fulton's alter egos.

In time, everything falls into place and after a while Jack and I became comparatively happy at home with the family. Funnily enough, I then hated going to visit theatre dressing rooms. Remembering my own theatre life, I didn't take kindly to friends popping in to say hello during the show. It's so off-putting. So I never subjected my fellow artists to the same.

I did like to go and see the dress rehearsal of the latest pantomime at the Pavilion, before the opening night. I would get a chance to sum up the merits of the show and wallow in a bit of nostalgia.

At this point in our lives, Jack was doing winter seasons at the Glasgow Pavilion, and summer seasons at the Gaiety in Ayr, so we had the best of both worlds. Jack was home for the winter and family holidays were spent in Ayr. Incidentally, Jack starred in eighteen Pavilion pantomimes and never had a formal contract. He simply had lunch at Glasgow's supremely elegant Rogano restaurant, shook hands with the managing director Mr. Fries Ballantine, and that was that, a gentleman's agreement. Not to be recommended, but it was Jack's way. He was always a bosses' man, always on time, knew his lines, and expected everyone around him to do the same.

In those early years we didn't socialise very much. Jack was a very private man, loved his home, television and a good read at the papers. And he loved his garden.

Fortunately, I was not enthusiastic about giving dinner parties. I liked to go to them but never felt up to giving one myself. I didn't have the confidence, as I was such a plain cook. And Jack was not a good host. He had to have a couple of drinks before the guests arrived, to overcome his shyness, and was always glad when our turn was over.

I read that Cilla Black was the same, could face any audience, but please, do not ask her to arrange a dinner party for ten! I know exactly how she felt. We are all excellent at some things, and not so good at others.

I may have been a reticent hostess but after being at home with the children for a few years, I looked forward to a short Christmas stint back in the spotlight. Later, whilst working at the Pavilion, Jack had the splendid idea of using Diana and I at the end of the panto to do a little novelty act, a family trio if you like. Jack was resplendent in his kilt and Diana and I had identical, beautiful blue dresses and wore white fur stoles. We did a few gags, I sang 'South American Joe', which Jack loved and I hated, and Diana sang 'Walking Back to Happiness', Helen Shapiro's big hit.

Diana did well but never had any notion of having a stage career. I'm happy to say she now runs a very successful business of her own and she was always first in her class at the local comprehensive school. I'd say, 'Have you no homework?' and she'd say, 'Yes, but I did it on the bus coming home.' Near her school leaving age, I thought it would be good for her to go to a private school, so she could choose what sort of education she would go on to. So off she went in her new uniform to Craigholme School for Girls, which she hated.

It was an all girls' school and she had been used to the fun of a mixed school. I had the best of intentions but I realise now that it's cruel to do that to a child so late in their schooling. Anyway, after much soul searching, she finished her education at her comprehensive, with the Headmaster's words ringing in my ears, 'She is university fodder you know, Mrs. Milroy.' And that she was. Diana has brains she hasn't even used yet.

When the kids were younger, my best friend Mary Slaven and I had a wee ploy to pass the afternoon till it was time to pick them up from school. We'd look in the paper, see what houses were for sale in the district and, with no intention of buying, we'd go for a viewing. Nine times out of ten, we got 'a cuppa tea and a fairy cake', too. We would leave the lady of the house with a 'You'll be hearing from us,' and chat on the way home, saying things like 'I didn't fancy her carpet' or 'Those curtains were lovely.'

One day, however, our weekly look took us to Ralston Avenue in Crookston. We viewed a lovely old detached stone villa with a magnificent garden. This one took my eye seriously. It needed a lot doing to it but I could see the potential.

I telephoned my lawyer Mr. William Allan, and we began negotiations. It had four bedrooms, three public rooms, and a large kitchen, perfect for a family. Not long after, we moved in. This really was my dream house. It was a labour of love to update and we had some fine BIG parties there! Catered, of course.

The cast of every show Jack was appearing in came to this lovely old house and the happiest evenings were Thursdays, my parents' weekly visit. I would go up for them and drive them down for our evening ritual. Isa always wore her good coat, a fur coat I had bought her years before, which she cared for and treasured. She never wore make-up, but she had the nicest skin I've ever seen on a woman, and the sweetest face. And Willie, with his baggy trousers and white, open necked shirt, was a fine figure of a man.

Anna Cowie, my life long friend in show business, would often come along too. A pianist, she was well tuned in to my parents. We always had tea, salmon and cucumber sandwiches and cakes. No 'wee sensations' – we didn't need them.

Then Anna would say, 'What do you want to sing Willie?' and every week it was 'The Song that Reached My Heart.' Soon Isa would take over on the piano and play beautifully on the black notes. Where this came from I don't know. But she was good. Later on I would bring the tape recorder in and she'd let me interview her, pretending she was a film star. She would break into helpless laughter, tears running down her cheeks, unable to speak for laughing.

Jack was very fond of Isa. He'd go into her wee kitchenette to wash the dishes after a meal, and one time she caught him throwing out a saucer full of peas and another of beans. She cried, 'My God, son, that's Willie's dinner tomorrow!' We had no fridges in those days, just a cool pantry.

Isa would make Jack hamburger and chips and he'd kid her along saying, 'What's this you're giving me Isa?' She would reply, 'That's the best of Galbraith's hamburgers!' And the laughter would start up again.

She was a joy to be with and, of course, my visits to her were endless. I'd take Jim with me and if she didn't want him to hear what we were talking about she'd say, 'Mary, there's a big hole in the wall!' and poor Jim would be sent off out the room on some pretext or other. On the way home he'd say, 'I didn't see any holes in my gran's wall.' Isa had them all conned. She was definitely the commander from the couch.

As I remember, it was while we were still in the little house in Hatton Gardens that the crowning highlight of Jack's career, 'Francie and Josie', began to glimmer. We met Rikki Fulton at a party thrown by Jimmy Logan. Rikki invited us to supper at his flat in Byres Road, where he lived with his first wife Ethel. Wee Alex Finlay and his wife Rita made up the party. It was a happy night, though no business was discussed – we just had lots of fun.

It transpired that Rikki had been watching Jack's work at the Ayr Gaiety and liked his style. He asked Jack to join him for the next summer show at the King's Theatre in Edinburgh, the legendary Howard and Wyndham 'Five Past Eight' series. Jack was over the moon. He was glowing once again and living up to the title of 'he of the beautiful face', with smart suits and all the best trimmings of the business. This was real class, the number one glamour 'gig' in Scotland in 1960. I was so proud of him, and loosened my grip on being his sidekick and concentrated on my home and family, and not before time.

Ethel Scott, Rikki's first wife, was the comics' feed in the 'Five Past Eight' shows. She worked with both Jack and Rikki. I took to Ethel immediately. She was the best feed, had a great sense of humour, and could be very glamorous when called upon. She used to say to me, 'Mary, I thought you would be coming round backstage to show me how you worked with Jack,' and she meant it genuinely.

Many a happy party I joined at their home after the show.

Ethel would have made a splendid interior decorator. Her eye for colour and décor was stunning. She was small, dark, very pretty and a damned good performer.

Ethel, Clem Ashby and Rikki made an excellent comedy team but I have to tell you that I had no idea that Ethel and Rikki were not happily working and enjoying life together, and I was sad when I heard that their marriage was over, but at that point I only knew them both socially and on those occasions they would naturally put up a solid front.

It was quite some time before I was aware that Rikki had met his new lady, Kate, but of course I was happy for him. And she proved to be his soul mate for the rest of his days, so it turned out to be a happy decision for him to marry Kate.

Talking about changing spouses, I laugh when I look back on an incident that took place during the 'Five Past Eight' run. We had just moved to our lovely new home in Crookston and I was heavily into the process of redecoration. Jim was on his school holidays, aged seven, and not doing my nervous system any good by being around during the house-beautiful bit. So I said to Jack, 'Be a pal and take Jim through to Edinburgh with you, while I get on with things in the house.'

Jack was happy to have him and off they trotted, bags packed for the big adventure. When they came home on the

Sunday I asked Jim if he was enjoying his wee holiday. And Jim replied, 'Yes, Auntie Eileen, Daddy and I are having a great time.'

'Who the hell is Auntie Eileen?' I said to Jack.

He blushed like a baby. He had taken Eileen, who was the principal dancer in the show, to have lunch every day. And why not? Nobody's perfect, and I soon saw the funny side because I knew full well there was nothing in it. Jack Milroy would have run a mile if anyone had come on to him seriously. I subsequently met the girl and she was nice and I'm sure Jack had a happy time.

During the run, Rikki said to Jack that he was thinking of doing a sketch for the show featuring two Glasgow teddy boys and would he be interested in doing it? And Jack said, 'Why not?' Rikki went straight out and bought the suits, Jack bought the wigs . . . and a legend was born. They did a twenty minute long 'Francie and Josie' sketch for two summers in a row and it always brought the house down.

Then Rikki was offered a series for Scottish Television. He proposed doing six half-hour shows, 'The Adventures of Francie and Josie', incorporating the stage sketches, and STV readily agreed. The public loved them and as Jack often said, 'It was like taking sweeties off a wean.'

After they recorded the first show, we went on holiday. When we returned, the very first show had gone out. It was 1963 and it was an instant success. After just three episodes, the viewing figures were enormous.

The story goes that the children were the first to cotton on to it. The shows went out at 6.30pm, the kids loved them, told their parents, and soon everybody was watching. If parents wanted their kids to come in the house, they just had to open the window and call 'Francie and Josie are on the telly' and in they would rush.

Half the wee boys in Glasgow were walking around doing

the famous 'Francie and Josie' walk . . . do you remember that gallus swagger? And people started saying 'Hullawrerr' instead of 'hello'. It was great having such an immediate, warm reaction.

I knew what recognition show business could give but this was something else . . . instant stardom! Though Jack said it didn't really hit home to HIM until one afternoon in Airdrie, when it dawned on him that he and Rikki really were famous!

They had been invited to declare a large new electrical goods store open – pretty routine stuff they thought. A jeep was waiting to drive them into the town centre in their red and blue suits and the famous wigs and, as they drew nearer to the main square, they were surrounded by a huge crowd. Even with four policemen surrounding the jeep they could barely move. There were literally thousands of fans surging forward and shouting 'shake my hand, Francie . . . shake my hand, Josie.'

When Rikki leaned over the side of the jeep and DID shake someone's hand, he was dragged off, and disappeared into the crowd. Two policemen had to rescue him!

The scene was amazing and the sheer crush of the crowd surging forward knocked in the windows of the new store. Jack said they were like royalty arriving, complete with police escort, and that was when the penny finally dropped for him about how popular they were.

By then, they had been on TV for two years and had reached audiences in Scotland, the Borders and Northern Ireland. We couldn't go shopping without Jack being followed for autographs. And we couldn't go on holiday as a normal family would because no sooner had we settled ourselves round a pool abroad than someone would come up and say, 'Howzit goan Francie?'

Or, when we came home, there would be a knock on the front door and there would be two wee boys saying, 'Is Francie coming out?' and I'd say, 'He's away at his Auntie Jessie's.'

One day the telephone rang and lo and behold it was STV offering me a small part in one of the Francie and Josie episodes. My first reaction was, 'My, fancy someone remembering me!' Don't forget I'd been out of show business for quite a few years by this time. Then the terror struck! Could I still produce the goods? Jack didn't know anything about the offer, but of course I said yes, signed the contract and had two days to work with Rikki and Jack.

I soon received my script and noted I was to be one of the two girlfriends of the duo – Una McLean being the other. I was glad that it was Una. She was so clever and always good for a laugh, but you know a funny thing? I didn't enjoy it. It frightened the hell out of me. I'd never worked with Rikki Fulton and come to think of it, I hadn't done much television, so I was like a fish out of water. I just had a couple of lines – I could have telephoned it in – but it was still a struggle to get through the scene. I distinctly remember saying to Una McLean, 'Do you know something Una? I'd rather be at home making the mince'. It just wasn't my scene.

I didn't get asked to do any more episodes, so I have a good idea the feeling was mutual, but for Jack and Rikki, alias Francie and Josie, it was instant and enduring stardom.

Naturally, the kids and I saw very little of Jack during this time – there is always a price to pay for fame. Jack was just taking on too much work. He would rehearse and record 'Francie and Josie' at the studios then go over to the Pavilion and do two shows a night. Then there was the fact that he'd had nodules removed from his throat the previous year. He was in serious need of a proper rest.

So when he said, 'Mary, I want to go to London,' it was a case of 'stop the world, I want to get off'. He was over-tired and stressed and needed a change of scene.

Going to London was the last thing I wanted to do but I saw

that things were far from alright with Jack so we uprooted the kids, sold the house and made for the capital. Strangely enough, from that dodgy start, the next two years were the happiest of my life. I had 'Francie' all to myself, the kids had their daddy and Jack began his life long love affair with the bookies.

I think it was the move to London and the chance to lead a more normal life that prevented Jack having a breakdown.

13

THE CAPITAL LIFE

When we arrived in London we took an apartment in a block of flats called the Water Gardens, very elegant and not a stone's throw from Marble Arch. It had a split level lounge and dining-room and one full wall of windows leading out to a lovely balcony. I was happy there, but my itchy feet caught up with me again and I enrolled at the main Pitman's College in Southampton Row for a crash course in shorthand and typing. Don't ask me why, but I fancied being a secretary.

Maybe it was some residual memory from when I took secretarial studies at Lambhill Street School. Jack laughed, 'Mary, you won't last a week!' But I stuck it out for a year, and I noticed that Jack tucked away my shorthand and typing certificates, so I think he was secretly proud of my willingness to try new things.

When I left the college I perused the *Evening Standard* to get myself a job. I thought 'director's secretary or nothing.' I actually joined the Belgravia Bureau in Knightsbridge, adjacent to Harrods. I was in charge of the nanny/mothers help section, a job that had no boss, which suited me fine. The telephone was my master, and rang incessantly.

I interviewed the girls and ladies, checking out their references and arranging meetings with their prospective employers. We didn't charge the girls we placed, we billed the client. I had a right royal time there. I used my typing all the time, and my shorthand skills came in handy to take notes over the telephone.

Sian Phillips was one of my nicest customers. At that time she was married to Peter O'Toole, the film star. When I fixed her up with a nanny, I always received a telephone call to thank me personally. Truly a nice woman, who excelled in her brilliant Dietrich homage show to the great Marlene in the West End a few years ago and toured with it all over the country. She contrived to look uncannily like the great star.

It was a happy job, but very demanding, and every Friday I would say to Jack, 'I'm jacking this in.' Then I'd change my mind on the Monday.

There is something about browsing through Harrods in your lunch hour that is very appealing. And sometimes Jack would drive down and we would lunch together in one of those charming little pubs that London does so well. This was the 'Swinging Sixties' and Jack would give marks out of ten to the passing 'swinging chicks' while we snacked. He loved it all and was learning to relax and enjoy life.

There were lots of wealthy Americans living in the Water Gardens, over working in the capital representing oil companies. And George Raft, then very big in gangster movies, always playing the suave hoodlum, lived there. I never met Raft, but we were assured that his car was parked next to mine in the underground car park.

Living in London brought back memories of my early days as a singer with the dance bands of the Thirties. I vividly recall finishing the second house at say, the Holborn Empire, getting out of my stage clothes and going back down to the stage, where the musicians were arranged in a circle, with the microphone centre stage. Then we would record a half-hour programme to be broadcast from Radio Luxembourg finishing around one o'clock in the morning. This happened once a week, and I never received a penny piece in addition to my usual weekly wage, but no doubt Roy Fox was laughing all the way to the bank.

Radio Luxembourg started up in 1933 and broadcast into the 1990s. Names like Noel Edmonds, Jimmy Saville, David Jacobs, Scotland's Stuart Henry and many more, presented programmes and honed their broadcasting skills on the station.

Yes, London brought back echoes of my salad days with the big orchestras and if I'd had the good sense to try to put my foot into the London recording scene again it would surely have been to my advantage. But everything is rosy in retrospect and it wasn't to be for me. I thought it was all too long ago for it to be a viable proposition.

And anyway, I was really happy in London. I had Jack all to myself there, which meant everything to me.

But there are always problems, even in Paradise. We went on holiday to the south of France and on our return to the Water Gardens discovered that our flat had been well and truly 'turned over'. All my clothes were in a heap. Even my Hoover was ripped open to see if I had hidden any jewels inside it. It really is a rotten feeling to know that a stranger has had a good rumble through your home. I shouted to Jack, 'Oh my God, they've pinched my mink and they've got Bessie.' Bessie was an old beaver fur coat I'd had since the flood, much worn and much loved. They had taken a beautiful mink Jack had bought me. But no, at least we found old Bessie at the bottom of the heap of clothes. They knew what they were after. That is the only time in my life I have been burgled.

During our London sojourn Jack had made several forays back up to Scotland. He did a season at the King's Theatre in Edinburgh with the Alexander Brothers who were just coming to the fore with their 'Nobody's Child' hit. The show was a roaring success and Jack, who was putting it on himself, made a great deal of money.

When he came back down to London he had big ideas. 'This

is it, Mary. You produce your own shows and make a fortune,' he enthused.

The following year he went back up to Edinburgh, put the show on again with a different cast, and lost the lot!

Between that and my mink trauma – it didn't take much persuasion – we were glad to come home to Glasgow, where all we had known was kindness. We found an elegant flat in the city's West End and I resumed my show business career. The kids were grown by now and after our first summer season Jim was off to boarding school at Rannoch, close to Gordonstoun, Prince Charles' old school.

I can sense you thinking, 'Aye, Mary, it's a long way from Kinning Park'. And it was. God was good to the Milroys, but both of us had backgrounds that helped us keep our feet firmly on the ground.

We fixed a summer season at the Barrfield's Pavilion in Largs and took a bungalow for the duration. Our son Jim was given the job of lime boy and his task was the follow spot. This meant that when an artist walked onstage, Jim had to follow him or her with the spotlight. He did this beautifully for everyone else, but when I came on, he used to leave ME in a blackout!

The cast included a very young Paul Young whose mother Freddie, then a well known theatrical agent, had sent Paul down to Largs to learn his trade. I recall that even then, he was fishing mad. Paul used to take Jim and his pal out fishing and Jim would have the rod his 'uncle' Charlie had bought him. Charlie Sim, a star of Scottish Television's 'The One O'Clock Gang' show, was the kindest of men.

Paul learned to tap dance, work in sketches, do little 'front cloth' spots on his own, and was happy with us. Every Monday change of programme, his mum and dad would come and see the show to see how he was getting on.

His dad, the late John Young, played the minister in Scottish

Television's soap, 'Take the High Road'. It is odd that for all his acting talents and the splendid shows and television programmes he has graced, it was his first love that brought Paul national fame, presenting his many fishing series.

Jack had loads of new material he had been working on whilst I was at home, so I was excused writing duties. It was a beautiful summer and we all gave the famous Nardini's ice cream parlour a walloping. Even writing about it makes my mouth water.

When the summer was nearing its end, we took Jim up to Rannoch to begin his first term and went on to the Glasgow Pavilion to do an autumn show. My mother had missed us while we were in London but had written long and interesting letters to me every week. And by this time my father had retired from Shell Mex and was living happily at 300 Talla Road. He loved his garden and the sunshine. At the first blink of sun, off came his shirt.

During that season I was up having an afternoon visit, and my mother suddenly said, 'Take me to the window Mary.' I thought this was an odd request but went along with it. She had always loved her garden and enjoyed looking out at it. She stood for a long time looking at it without speaking and finally I said, 'Are you all right, mother?'

I had no response so I walked her back to her chair and called the doctor. She had suffered a massive stroke, and she never spoke to me again.

My brother Eddie and I were in an awful state, he more than I was, as he had been closer to her during all the years I was off on my travels. We had private nurses for her day and night and eventually she was taken in to the Southern General Hospital. On one visit my sister-in-law Renee said to me, 'Have you seen your mother's leg?'

I looked, and knew it was gangrenous. The doctors advised us it would have to be amputated. They had to try to save lives. Eddie and I went to see her just after she had been given the 'pre-med'. She opened her eyes, looked straight at Eddie and spoke the only words I heard her say during her illness, 'Oh, my big sailor boy.'

The day after next, she died.

All during mother's illness I worked in the Pavilion show. I had no option, but in retrospect it was probably the best thing for me – occupational therapy.

Mother had a wee sixpenny-a-week policy with the Pearl Insurance, but I thought, 'I have enough money to do the funeral properly for her.' But do you know, that little policy did the lot, even covering the nice meal for her friends afterwards. The older generation always made sure that they left enough to 'see them off' without being beholden to anyone. That was just what my mother had done.

It was my father's wish to stay in their family home and he made a damn good job of it. My mother would have been proud of him.

14

A CAT NAP THROUGH CANADA AND A WEE NIP AND TUCK

Jack and I were invited by Andy Stewart to do a tour of Canada and America in 1970. It was just what I needed to brighten my spirits after the death of my mother. My Dad was okay and my brother Eddie was going to keep an eye on him while we were out of the country. So we got ready for the off.

The cast comprised Calum Kennedy, Sally Logan and Joe Gordon, Jack Milroy and Mary Lee, and Ken Haynes, a fine pianist who went on to Radio Clyde 2's 'Ken's Ceilidh' fame. Ken was great fun and had a wicked sense of humour.

It was always tiring on tour. After each show, there was always a meal with the committee of whatever club we had entertained, and I would be dead tired and put on my shades and snooze during the speeches.

Our first port of call was Quebec. It felt odd when shop-keepers addressed you in French first before resorting to English. I wonder if they still do that? I loved Canada. It was such a calm and cultured country with so much to see . . . if you could keep awake.

We went to play a town near Niagara Falls and I was too tired to go and view them. This lethargy stayed with me all through the tour. We went by train through the Rocky Mountains, and I slept through the experience, going to the dining car at 7pm and asking, 'Have we come to the Rocky Mountains yet?' and the gang saying, 'We passed them three hours ago.'

We spent the night in Calgary with Canadian friends, who gave us a beautiful present, a bottle of whisky with a purple cover and tie string, then continued on our journey by plane. As we flew over the fruit growing region, which Jack called the Okey Dokey Valley – I can remember his gag but not the real name any more! – the plane suddenly began to shudder violently. We were in a huge thunderstorm, the turbulence was truly alarming and my first thought was, 'Oh no, is this it?'

Calum and Jack immediately asked the air hostess for a wee dram but she refused. Well, this was an emergency so they managed to get two paper cups and out came the purple bottle. I remember them saying that if we were going to go down, THEY would go with a wee dram in them! I often think of that dramatic flight, and what might have been.

At the end of the Canadian tour we moved on to America and our first taste of the States was Detroit, the car manu-facturing city. It was quite bewildering at first and to tell you the truth I didn't much like the feel of it. It was so fast and furious after the laid back Canadian attitudes.

The waitress in Detroit asked, 'You want coffee?' and you felt if you declined you would get the pot over your head! Eventually we hit New York and nothing, no nothing, beats your first time in the Big Apple! I loved the coffee shops with their endless supply of coffee, the cleanliness and the iced water. I have been back many times since, and I now love America.

When we had an evening off, Jack and I walked down Broadway. The pulse of this place was something else. I looked at the Palace Theatre and the statue of George M. Cohen. Broadway was tawdry, exciting and a one-off. Once you've been there you lose your heart to it forever. And by a lucky coincidence of planning, we were staying in a hotel called The Edison, just off Broadway.

I have never seen so many locks on a bedroom door. I had a Scottish friend who was living in New York and said to her, 'Are these locks to keep the burglars out?' She replied, 'No honey, it's to keep them in.'

The highlight of the tour was performing in Carnegie Hall. I stood quietly in the middle of the stage, looked around me, and thought, 'Judy Garland sang here.' Quite an experience.

It was not unlike our own King's Theatre in Glasgow, only MUCH bigger. We were only there for one night, but it was a night to remember. It was a long time ago, but it stands out like a jewel in my memory.

When the tour finished we arrived back in Glasgow and the plan was to have a holiday in Majorca. But my lethargy had returned with a vengeance and Jack said, 'Maybe you should get a check-up before we go.'

My consultant, Dr. Harper, paid a visit and said, 'Mary, I'm going to take you in to Stobhill Hospital. We'll do a wee D&C tomorrow.'

'Will I be okay for Monday?' I asked.

'Yes,' he said, and I happily went into hospital complete with false eyelashes and four inch heels. Off I went to theatre next morning saying, 'This is not the kind of theatre I'm used to.'

The next thing I knew, a nurse was bending over me saying, 'Here you! I've missed my lunch because of you.' Understatement of the year. I'd had a complete hysterectomy!

Jack was telephoned and informed. He didn't know what the hell I'd had done. He visited that evening and saw that I was okay. Well I LOOKED okay. Eventually he said, 'Mary, would you mind if I beetled off? There's a rare cowboy picture on at the Odeon.' Love's young dream, eh?

Later, a nurse caught me going to the loo with my four inch heels on and said, 'Take these off immediately.'

I said, 'The day you find me without my "high nancies" on, you can put me down!' I never took them off.

When I came home Jack was unfailingly good and kind to me, but it took me one long time to get back to square one. But when I did, I was ready to kick my height again, feeling much the better for the op. And it certainly explained why I'd felt so tired on tour.

I've no idea why, but when I was ready to get back to work, suddenly I didn't want to do comedy any more. I fancied going back to my roots and singing again. I had reached the age of fifty and Jack joked with me, 'Who wants a fifty-year-old chanteuse?'

But I am, and always have been, a very determined lady, and pushed on regardless. I stopped smoking, put on weight, and went on a diet. I got the weight off again, and to tidy things up, decided to have a facelift. I figured this fifty-year-old chanteuse was going to look her best before resuming her singing career and paid a visit to my very understanding doctor to make my request.

He didn't bat an eyelid and referred me to a Mr. Jackson, who consulted in very ordinary premises in Sauchiehall Street. There was no drama about it. This was a private job. Mr. Jackson agreed to do the business for me and I was to attend Canniesburn Hospital in about a fortnight's time. It was as simple as that. So you see, plastic surgery was on offer all these years ago. Mr. Jackson was a good looking young surgeon who attended all the serious road accident cases and repaired their poor damaged faces.

The big day dawned and Jack drove me to the hospital where the fun began. I had the operation the next day but when I woke up, feeling not too bad, I couldn't hear a thing.

I thought, 'This is God smiting me for being so vain!'

Mr. Jackson was not best pleased and said, 'I didn't make you deaf, Mary.' An ear doctor was sent for and as soon as he'd syringed my ears, all was well. I lay that night and listened to the ticking of the little clock beside my bed, so grateful that I could hear it.

I was heavily bandaged and my eyes were swathed for twenty-four hours. Unable to stand the wait, I peeped out from the bandages and checked. Yes, I could still see.

That night when a nice nurse put drops in my eyes she said, 'God help you, pet.' I must have looked a right mess and I thought, 'Well hell mend you, Mary. It's self-inflicted.'

I had my upper and lower eyelids done as well. I thought I might as well go the whole hog!

One week later, all the bandages were removed and Jack arrived to take me home, me wearing a turban and dark glasses (very Gloria Swanson) for the journey. It was like water off a duck's back to Jack. He thought I was daft, but as long as I was doing the suffering he put up with me. I went home to recuperate in the enormous apartment we had at that time. I hid in the top bedroom, which had a little balcony attached and would sit out there and get the air. The pain wasn't so bad, but I looked as though a fast train had hit me.

Slowly, however, the ugly duckling changed into a swan and I was so much better looking than before. Mr. Jackson had said he didn't want people to say that I looked younger. He wanted them to say, 'Don't you look well.' And they did. Mary belied her age for many a long year after the op and it is only now that the mask is beginning to slip, but my eyes are still lineless . . . so go for it, girls.

I know you'll maybe be wondering what that little lot set me back. Well, it was the princely sum of £500, which nowadays wouldn't get a pimple removed from your face.

I can only thank the man above, who was obviously keeping

an eye on my wellbeing. In the hands of a not-so-brilliant surgeon I might have had a botched operation, but I was lucky. My surgeon went on to become Professor Ian Jackson, who adopted a disfigured little South American boy, then spent years reconstructing his face.

Ian's brilliance and that journey were captured in 'The Boy David', a moving documentary made for television by Desmond Wilcox, the late husband of Esther Rantzen.

When David was about seven, Ian Jackson and his wife Marjory came to visit Jack and me in our dressing room at the Pavilion Theatre. And brought him along.

David had the most beautiful eyes I've ever seen on a child, but no nose.

Mr. Jackson was growing some flesh on David's forehead which, eventually, would become his new nose. Marjory had knitted a special little hat to cover the flesh and protect it from the elements.

When they arrived in my dressing room, the child held his arms out to me and I picked him up. With his beautiful personality, all thoughts of his wee nose were gone. He was just the perfect child and I could understand why they loved young David so much.

Wonderful people, the Jacksons live happily in America now.

So, that's the story of my nip and tuck, but be very careful if YOU feel the urge. I went like a lamb to the slaughter, but I was lucky and landed in safe hands, unlike all the tragic women one sees every other week nowadays in television programmes about botched plastic surgery.

Mr. Jackson's skilled work certainly gave me the confidence to do a new act, singing all my nostalgic old songs, like 'I'll Be Seeing You', 'Whispering', 'Room 504' and 'A Nightingale Sang in Berkeley Square'. I loved every minute of it. And to begin with, Jack didn't push me to do comedy, but inevitably,

I resumed both threads. But singing was my first love once again.

15

A TOUR 'DOWN UNDER'
AND A RECORD BREAKING SEASON

Around this time, Jack and I appeared in three pantomimes at the Pavilion. The first two were with our pals the Alexander Brothers and we started with the wonderfully titled 'Widow Crankie's Hanky Panky'. Jack and I played two dames, who married the boys at the end of the panto.

The last was 'The Three Musketeers'. The cast was the Alexander Brothers, Johnny Adams, Jinty McEwan, the Maclean Sisters, Company Policy, and Russel Lane. The producer was Billy Dunlop and I played a nurse looking after the Maclean Sisters, who were very young then but tremendously talented. Jack played one of the musketeers and the Alexanders played the other two. We had great times at the Pavilion Theatre. The Alexander Brothers were a joy to work with, brilliant performers, great fun to be with, and so popular with the punters.

Jack always got to the theatre about an hour and a half before the curtain rang up, while I used to run in about ten minutes before a show, slap some make-up on, then run down for the opening chorus.

'Why do you do that, Mary?' he would ask.

To which I'd reply, 'It makes the night go in quicker.' That was before the days when rules got more strict and you had to be seen to go into the theatre 'for the half' – thirty minutes before curtain up.

On stage, Jack was the hardest person to feed. Often he'd just go off at a tangent and leave you there, wondering when you could feed him the line and get back to the sketch. But every word that came out of that experienced mouth was brilliant.

Most comics liked to work 'line for line', but not Jack who was just a naturally funny man. The perspiration would be running down my back, waiting to get in my tuppence worth. But he was an experienced idiot, and you loved him all the more for it.

If a drunk heckled, Jack would say, 'Stop the baun' (stop the band) and say to the offending person, 'If you don't like the show, go to the box office and get your money back. There are weans here wanting to enjoy the pantomime.'

The audience would invariably shout, 'You're quite right, Jack!'

Then Jack would say, 'Start the baun' and the pantomime would go merrily on.

What a character he was . . . a real one off.

It wasn't difficult to see where Jack got that strong individuality from, either. I remember when his mum, Mary, came to see us perform, she would buy a ticket for the show, and at the end of the performance she would march down the stalls, tap the orchestra leader on the shoulder and say, 'Give this to my son.'

'This' would be a big brown paper parcel tied with string, with a large home made dumpling inside. She was funny old soul, but so loveable.

Jack would tell her, 'Mother, I would have arranged a box of your own to see the show.' But that wasn't Mary's style. She always paid for her seat, delivered her dumpling and went home.

At the end of the first panto, we had a night out at the Ashfield Club in Glasgow, run by the ever-generous (late) Jimmy Donald. During the evening the cabaret began, with my big pal the late Glen Daly as compere. I brought a couple of nice piano parts along, slipped them to the pianist, and Glen Daly introduced me.

For the first time, the Alexander Brothers heard Mary Lee doing her nostalgic act. Well, within days Jack and I were booked to go with the boys on a tour of Australia and New Zealand.

I was the only lady in the party, and it was a joy to do from beginning to end. The company was Tom and Jack (the Alexanders), Jack and Mary, and the fine Bobby Harvey band. The late Ross Bowie sent us over, and David Lean looked after us on the Australian side.

We flew from Prestwick and, apart from refuelling, the only time we got off the plane was in Calcutta. 'Oh lovely,' I thought when we landed. 'We can get off for a wee blow of fresh air.' My God, it was like stepping into an oven!

I went to the ladies room in the airport and it was quiet and clean, with ladies lying on the floor in cotton saris pulled over their eyes. Not something you would see back home but it was obviously a favourite way to cool down in the baking Indian heat.

The first class on Quantas Airlines was truly lovely. Desks for the businessmen and a lovely bar. A steward who recognised us said to my Jack, 'Come upstairs two at a time and have a drink.' But big Jack Alexander said, 'Don't tell the rest of them, and you and I'll go up four times!' Nice thought but he was only teasing of course – we all went up.

Jack Alexander's sense of humour was unfailing. He bought a toy koala bear on the first leg of the tour and said, 'Mary, I can't get this in my case, will you carry it for me?' And carry it I did, all the way back to London.

We finally arrived in Perth, Australia, and were granted three days off for good behaviour. It's the only town that truly sticks in my mind, because I had time to see it.

I remember Jack and I went to see Barbara Streisand in 'Funny Girl' and we ate in lovely restaurants.

The venue for our fourth night was truly splendid. Violinist Ian Powrie, who was living there at the time, had a splendid violin session with Bobby Harvey back at the hotel, after the show. The next venue, however, left much to be desired so it was not all beer and skittles but the company was smashing and we laughed all the way.

Incidentally, we only saw one kangaroo, and that one was dead!

You name a town or city, and we played it. It was an endless round of hotels, sound checks at the theatre, show, airports, and away again.

In Sydney, we played in a lovely venue, and the city had an American 'feel' to it. In fact, the whole of Australia reminded me of America. At the airport, when we were leaving for the New Zealand leg of our tour, I saw so many families crying. We were so used to travelling and I said to Jack, 'Why are they all crying?'

And he said, 'Mary, some of the older ones perhaps really are saying goodbye.'

We flew from Sydney to Auckland, and when we arrived at the airport there were hula girls singing and dancing, and the pilots were like film stars.

'This is going to be beautiful,' I thought. In fact the hula dancers were there to meet their pals coming in from the islands to look for work.

When we arrived in Auckland itself, it was a Sunday night, and I tell you, the difference from Sydney was a culture shock. Auckland reminded me of Glasgow on a Sunday night. And, don't forget, I'm talking about three decades ago!

No doubt Auckland is swinging now, just as Glasgow is buzzing and beautiful, but to me, at that time, New Zealand was like a very old-fashioned Scotland and it felt like stepping back in time. I recall talking to some teenagers who were not dressed very trendily, and remarking, 'I thought you'd have lovely sweaters with all these sheep about.' To which they replied, 'No, it's all exported.' End of story.

I had a friend out there and she travelled 400 miles by car to see me. They think nothing of distance. She and her kids saw the show, stayed overnight, and drove back the 400 miles. A long way to see a show.

We did our final performance in Dunedin, roughly translated as old Edinburgh, took a photograph of the statue of Rabbie Burns in the square, and made for the airport and the long journey back to Scotland.

Back home, we began rehearsals for a Jack Milroy 'special' on television, which was to be done at the MacRobert Centre in Stirling. Jack worked with the late John Mulvaney, a little gem of a man. We did one of Jack's classic sketches, the wee boy on the train going to visit his granny. John played the ticket collector and I played a woman of the world who fancied the boy on the train who was big for his age. You can tell where it was all leading! I still have a video of the show, and I think I look rather nice as the very English lady, flirting with the boy. It's always nice to look at old film of oneself.

Jack was also invited to do a series for Scottish Television, which unfortunately was not well received by the public. It was a variety show, and the guest artists included Jackie Trent, one half of the well known singer/songwriters Tony Hatch and Jackie Trent, who wrote Petula Clark's mega hit 'Downtown' and the theme song for the Australian television soap, 'Neighbours'. Jackie was the nicest of lasses, very down to earth.

I appeared on three of the shows, though as I've said before, I didn't really like television work when it's not live. There's too much hanging about, and you do so many run-throughs that you're jiggered before you do the actual show. I often wonder if the men in the box who give the orders and say, 'We'll do that one from the top again,' realise how damn tired the artist is. To my mind, if you do the same gags over and over in the day they lose a lot of their freshness . . . even the crew don't laugh any more. But if you can't stand the heat, keep out of the kitchen.

I prefer off-the-cuff television, when you just chat. During the winter of the first pantomime at the Pavilion with the Alexander Brothers, Dorothy Paul invited me on to her daily lunchtime show 'Housecall' on Scottish Television. She and I chatted away, then I sang a medley of songs. Dorothy was a splendid interviewer and presenter. She is a star now, and nobody deserves her success more.

Learning material off by heart was never for me, not because I'm lazy, just because I don't have the sort of retentive memory you need for that kind of work. Jack and I used to take our respective scripts and he'd say, 'Learn the first five pages, Mary.' So we'd go to separate rooms and after a while I'd be the one with the sureness of mind to think I knew it all. We would join forces again, and Jack would say, 'Right, begin.' Jack would rattle the whole thing off with his photographic memory, and I'd stop at the end of the first page and 'dry'. The swear words that came out of my wee mouth were to be heard to be believed. I had such a struggle to learn, but once I had finally mastered it, the script was there for the rest of the pantomime.

In the summers of these years we worked with the 'boys' as we fondly called them, the Alexander Brothers. We appeared at the Eden Court Theatre in Inverness and Her Majesty's in Aberdeen, not forgetting a wonderfully successful summer season at the Gaiety Theatre in Ayr. It was a sweltering hot summer and Jack and the 'boys' broke all records.

There was never a seat to be had, absolutely packed for about five months.

The producer was the late Bruce McClure, who always called me 'Madam'. I marched down for his Highland glen finale resplendent in four inch high heels and tartan stockings. I hated flat shoes because I'm so small – you could kick me under the bed and not miss me. So I always chanced my arm, but Bruce would say, 'Get these high heels off, Madam.'

And I did, for the second house.

He'd then watch wee Mary with tears of laughter running down his face and afterwards he'd come into the dressing room and say, 'It's okay, Madam. Put on your stilts.'

Bruce was so easy to work with. He got the best out of you, and we fought the bit out with the easy banter of two people who liked each other. I miss him. He was very fond of his mother, and she could have knocked the socks off Hedda Hopper with her big hats.

Bruce told me a lovely story of a visit to Elton Johns' house in Los Angeles. He was left to sit by the pool and the telephone rang. It was Elizabeth Taylor. He was so excited, he nearly dropped the phone into the water. He also turned off the heat in Elton's pool, thinking to save him money as the day was so hot. He got hell when they all returned, as the pool was freezing.

I remember Bruce saying, 'Mary, you should see my house in London. It has a lovely Jacuzzi and I often sit there and think how I used to have an outside lavvy.' He was the best companion, and a true friend.

The next three years of our lives, from 1977 to '79 were to be spent at the Pavilion Theatre in Glasgow, with a very young Allan Stewart. He was so popular with the girls. There were always great screams when he came on. Just the shot in the arm the panto needed. That boy was to become like a second son to Jack and myself.

I played Flora the Forest Fairy and the whole script was in rhyme. I had lines stuck on the mirror, stuck on my hand, stuck anywhere there was room. There's no continuity in rhyme, and, thank goodness, I've never done it since.

In the second panto with Allan, I played the Queen. I liked that, plenty of dancing and singing. Jack played the dame.

The third year, Jack and I played the Ugly Sisters.

It's a hard part to play, because you have to be funny in your own spots, and then get the kids to boo when Cinderella doesn't get her ticket to the ball. Fiona Kennedy played Cinderella and was so talented and pretty.

Jack always said the best Pavilion panto he ever did was one he thought up himself – 'The World of Widow Kranky' in 1974. Jack played the Dame, in charge of eight orphan children. And that was when he discovered a wee lassie called Janette.

He featured her singing and dancing to the tune of 'Baby Face,' and anybody with half an eye could see she was a star in the making. And Janette and her husband Ian did indeed become famous. When they started out, Janette took their Krankies stage name from the pantomime. She said to Jack, 'I hope you don't mind, but we've pinched the name.'

That show was such a success it ran twice nightly, with THREE shows on a Saturday, from December until April!

Can you guess where Jack got the idea?

Every year we went down in the autumn to see all the London shows, but for some reason 'The Sound of Music' was into its fifth year at the Palace Theatre by the time we caught it. Jack thought, 'Why not have a Dame in charge of children,' and that was the germ of the idea for the panto. He picked the songs and thought up the ideas for the script.

Jan Currie worked with us on the shows and was the finest Principal Boy I've ever seen. She used to say to me, 'No more show business for me, Mary. I'm going into management.' And she did. She went on to become one of the most prestigious agents in London, after taking over the Billy March agency.

Many years on, Allan Stewart telephoned Jack and I to tell us he was taking over from Brian Connelly in 'The Jolson Story' show.

I said, 'But you've got a light voice, son.'

So immediately I got the full works, 'April Showers' and he was Jolson to a tee.

We flew down to London to see his show. Allan was absolutely brilliant, and so shy about his achievements. We were popped back to our hotel in his magnificent car and lunched the next day with Allan and his lovely wife Jane and their kids.

We were truly, truly proud.

At the Pavilion, Allan used to throw marvellous last night parties. The night always began for him when Jack turned up in some ludicrous outfit, and kept them all laughing. There's a shyness about Allan which is very endearing.

These years started a friendship with Allan and his family which lasts to this very day. I now have the pleasure of seeing his lovely shows at the King's Theatre in Edinburgh every Christmas and he never passes my door without coming up for a wee plate of his Aunty Mary's soup.

16

FRENCH LEAVE
AND FAMILY HEARTBREAK

Jack and I would sometimes take summers out and headed for our favourite spot, Juan Les Pins in the South of France. We had a beautiful apartment there in the Edin Residence, on the sea front. We motored all the way down, and when we got to France I would say, 'Now remember, you drive on the right now.' And then I'd say, 'When am I going to take over?' But when Jack let me, I nearly had a Charlie. What speed, and if you weren't quick enough, they'd honk you off the road. It would have put the fear of God into you.

I loved airing my French and have always wanted to be fluent. I know I never shall, but I get by.

We always went to France in late September, when the place was very chic. Jack and I both loved the Côte D'Azur. Ladies with pink hair and poodles to match. Beautiful boutiques, and the sand was combed to perfection. One year, we went in August, and the French were all down for a spree from Paris. The place was awash with candy floss and it wasn't the same place at all.

No matter where I went, I always had my radio and my recorder. I'd pass many a dull afternoon recording stuff and listening back. It was the beginning of another career which was to happen many years later.

I didn't tell you that quite a few years earlier, I lost my father. I think it's a subconscious wish not to remember because it hurts to remember dear old Wullie. He lived till he was 81 in his 300 Talla Road house, with two budgies he let fly out of their cage. They were happy, but my mother would not have approved. I used to love to go up at nights and make his tea and play chequers with him.

He'd say, 'Did you let me win?' I'd say, 'No, honest, father. You won fair and square.' Then the boxing would come on and his chair would come up to the telly, and he didn't notice anything else. I'd go into his kitchen and give it a good clean, and prepare his meal for the next night. He was a tidy man, but it needed a woman's touch once a week.

Jack was doing a pantomime with Rikki Fulton that year, which was 1972, so I was there to look after Wullie. My father suffered a heart attack and we lost him.

At his funeral, my ex-neighbour Chrissie Dunsmore urged me, 'Sing for your daddy, Mary. Sing along with the hymns.' But if you had paid me a million pounds, I couldn't have sung that day. I was utterly devastated.

And do you know, for long enough after his death, I'd be sitting on the stage singing a slow song and I'd feel his hand on my shoulder. It wasn't in any way frightening. In fact, it felt reassuring. And it went on for as long as it took for me to heal.

I still have vivid memories of my fathers' parents. His mother was a beautiful woman and his father was very distinguished, always wore a long, well-groomed beard, and a night cap in bed. At least, that is MY memory of them.

I don't know how true it is, but I remember being told that my grandfather walked into Glasgow on his own at the age of fourteen, possibly from one of the outlying farms, got himself a job and stayed in the city from that day on.

When I was about ten-years-old I used to visit my grand-parents every Sunday night. My grandfather was bed bound by then but he was an extremely clever old man and used to take my lessons every Sunday.

One night, I had done extremely well and he hugged me. Well, I was out of the door like a shot, because I got such a fright. His beard had tickled me! It has to be said that we were not a demonstrative family, and this was simply a generous gesture because I had done so well. My mother was mortified and made me come back to say 'sorry' for upsetting Papa McDevitt.

Earlier on, I introduced you to my wee brother Eddie.

He was three-and-a-half years younger than me and never let me forget the half!

When Eddie suffered a stroke it was no hardship to me to visit him. In fact I loved spending time with him, because he never lost his sense of humour. To other patients he would say, 'This is my sister, she's older than me,' then he would laugh.

We always kept that up.

There was a fellow patient in the ward who said to him, 'Is that Aunty Mary Lee?' referring to the 'character' I later assumed for my Radio Clyde show, and when Eddie said indeed it was, the patient said, 'Well I think she's a bloody bampot.'

Eddie said to me, 'If I could get out of this bed, I'd mark his cards.'

'Eddie, the man's right,' I said. 'I AM a bloody bampot,' and we both laughed heartily.

Each time I came in to the ward he would say, 'Do your wee dance,' and I'd do the step Barbara Streisand did in 'Funny Girl.'

Eddie was like myself, ever young. If someone said, 'Great film on this afternoon. Betty Grable is in it,' HE would say, 'Who is Betty Grable?'

When my son went to boarding school Eddie called him 'Prince Charles'. He was naturally funny, and that's a rare gift. He wasn't the star of the family but he shone in my eyes.

Eddie was a keen bowler and much loved by his club members. One day his wife Renee telephoned me and simply said, 'We've lost Eddie,' and a light went out of my life. He was such a handsome big fellow, a six-footer who loved sport and was a judo instructor.

So, I am the last of our family. I often wish I'd had a sister, someone of your own to go into town with or have a natter on the telephone with, but it wasn't to be.

I have written about my parents and wee Eddie, but not a lot about my own children because I want to protect their privacy. This is Jack's and my story, and it is only right and proper to keep it that way.

Talking about my family reminds me of another important member. My father had a brother called John, who lived to be 101. At the end of his life he was cared for at Erskine Hospital, which is on the outskirts of Glasgow, established to look after ex-servicemen and a painting of my uncle hangs as you go into the main hall.

Resplendent in the kilt, Jimmy Logan once took a party of us to entertain at Erskine Hospital to mark that years' V.E. Day anniversary, and I was proud to be shown Uncle John's portrait during our visit.

We owe so much to these men who fought for us in the last war – when will we ever learn?

17

BIG BAND DAYS AND
BABES IN THE WOOD

On our regular holidays to London, Jack and I would always go to see shows. On one trip I said to Jack, 'I should ring Alan Dell,' he of the beautiful voice, who presented 'The Big Band Days' from BBC Broadcasting House. Alan used to play my re-recorded waxings with the Roy Fox band on his radio show.

We duly presented ourselves at Broadcasting House to visit him and it suddenly occurred to me that I didn't know what Alan looked like . . . but I recognised the voice, of course. He took me through to a dubbing studio, and we recorded our casual blether, with me telling him what I was up to. He spliced the conversation and used it on many of his broadcasts, especially if he was playing a 'Little Mary Lee' record. Alan often played 'Nice Work If You Can Get It'.

It really does show that you can't sit back in this life and wait for things to happen. You have to get out there and hustle.

The follow up to this meeting with Alan was an invitation to sing at the London Festival Hall, in a Big Band show. I sent a tape of the songs I wanted to do, and Alan had the orchestrations done.

What a joy the show was. Jack couldn't come with me as he was booked to do an after-dinner speech that evening, so off I toddled on my own. I even met two of the original Roy Fox musicians.

And who was in the audience? He of the Rolls Royce and Savile Row suits – yes, Roy Fox himself.

Henry Hall was also present and Syd Lawrence and his band did the second half of the show. Alan Dell introduced us in his inimitable style, and the entire show was broadcast. It was indeed a night to remember.

The Festival Hall is a one off, not unlike our Royal Concert Hall in Glasgow. The audience is behind you, to the side of you and very much in front of you and the atmosphere was electric.

That night renewed my friendship with Roy Fox. So much water had flown under the bridge since I last saw him. We fell into a nice easy friendship and when I visited London I used to look him up in his Chelsea flat, off the King's Road. I'd bring the biscuits, and he'd provide the coffee.

One day I said, 'Roy, would you mind if I brought my tape recorder, and we could tape a wee blether?'

'Sure, honey, that would be nice,' he replied.

I recorded the most marvellous chat with Roy Fox, reminiscing about his young days in Santa Monica. He told me how his people had been in the Salvation Army, and he had played with their band as a boy. He even touched on his romance with Jean Harlow, the original Hollywood goddess and assured me that Jean had been a Boston socialite. He talked about watching the Keystone Cops in action, filming on the beach, when he was a boy. Later, he conducted a band for the Fox Studios which played while the silent movies were being made. Between shots, the extras would dance, whilst the next shot was being set up. Oh, and so much more. The tape is one of my rarest treasures.

Just a couple of years after these happy encounters, Roy Fox died.

Alan Dell invited me to sing again at the London Festival Hall in June, 1982. Part of the evening's entertainment was a tribute to honour Roy Fox's life and work and, of course, I was happy to do this.

Alan Dell asked the Mike Sammes' Singers to play 'The Cubs', the vocal trio in the Fox Orchestra and my dear friend Denny Dennis and I sang, 'Let's Call the Whole Thing Off.'

The section ended with the original concert arrangement of 'Whispering', for which I wore a copy of the original outfit I had worn with the band. It was a very sentimental evening, and I wouldn't have missed it for worlds.

Jack travelled to London with me and was happy to sit through rehearsals, but when the show proper came, he said, 'Mary, I'll just stand at the side and watch you from there.' I understood this, because I had attended so many of Jack's opening nights, and hated sitting through the show from the front, in case he would forget his lines.

It's just a case of the jitters, caused by being too close to the person involved. But all went well, and the show was broadcast.

In my more mellow moments, which are few and far between, I sit and listen to the 1982 recording, and can't believe that time has flown by so quickly.

The winter before the London Festival Hall show, I appeared with Jack and Rikki Fulton in pantomime at the King's Theatre in Edinburgh. Jack and Rikki had previously done three pantos together at the Glasgow Pavilion, then Rikki said he would like to go back to Edinburgh, but Jack stayed at the Pavilion and they went their separate ways for the following winter season.

However, Jack broke his 18-year run with the Pavilion when Rikki again suggested joining him in Edinburgh. They did

'The Sleeping Beauty', followed by 'Babes in the Wood', and I was happy to join in.

It was a great cast that I'll reel them off for you, and you'll see that 'Dr Show Business' has been good to them.

Ruth Madoc was the fine Principal Boy. The only time we hit the stage together was in the 'finding the babes' part, where we all went on with lanterns on a darkened stage. One night, she whispered to me, 'Mary, bach, I've done a pilot for a show called 'Hi-de-Hi'. Cross your fingers that I'll get it.'

Well of course she did, and made the part of Gladys her own.

Principal girl was my friend from the Pavilion pantomime, Fiona Kennedy, Calum's eldest daughter. Married now with three lovely children, Fiona still has a career. She is Mother Earth, and her door was always open to Jack and me.

The Robbers in this 'Babes in the Wood' were Gregor Fisher, alias Rab C. Nesbit, now a household name, and Tony Roper, also of Rab C. fame, who also featured in Scottish Television's tongue-in-cheek football quiz programmes as well as writing the immensely successful plays 'The Steamie' and 'Paddy's Market'.

I recall saying to him, 'You're too young to have lived in the steamie days, Tony!'

He replied, 'I used to go to my mammy's house and listen to her talk of the old days.' So from little acorns came the brilliant play 'The Steamie', now also a bestselling novel.

I auditioned for Tony for the London version of 'The Steamie', but he didn't think I was right for the part of Dolly. I don't blame him. I arrived for the audition with the obligatory false eyelashes and high heels!

I do wish Tony could have seen the 'uncut' version. All I had to do was think of my mother, the perspiration dripping from her, hanging her clothes on the pulley after a visit to the steamie. I would then have been on the right track for Dolly.

Lesson learned – don't let vanity get in the way of ambition.

Rikki and Jack starred as the Babes, and Rikki joked that they were the oldest Babes in the business! I played Wee Auntie Jessie and it was my first bash at playing Dame – Jack usually took that role.

He always laughed and told me folk never said, 'My, you were great in the panto.' They would say, 'You've got a rare pair of legs as a woman.' And he had.

Jim Byars was the 'baddie', and Company Policy were Robin Hoods' Band of Men, and fine looking lads they were, too. We had a good-looking chorus, both men and women.

Every principal was understudied, and mine, one of the singers, was always on the side of the stage learning the part. So I knew how Will Fyfe had felt when he asked me to remain in my dressing room. It puts you off, to say the least.

Of course she was only trying to learn in case of my being off. But oh God, principals are never off! That's why the lot of the understudy is so thankless. Show business is a tough world and we perform till we drop. I'm never sure why that is. Everybody knows the old adage about 'the show must go on . . .' but nobody is irreplaceable, so it would anyway.

Working with Jack and Rikki was great fun, which was just as well because we did the show twice daily, at 3pm and 7pm, and that is hard work. I enjoyed the show, but costume changes are tiring, especially when you have as many as twelve in one show. But at least they provided a dresser, which was nice. Mine was a great girl called Leone, a niece of Sean Connery.

I remember Rikki Fulton saying to me – 'Do you go out between shows Mary?'

I said, 'Yes. I go out for a meal and come back in time for the half'.

He said, 'Can I give you a bit of advice?'

I said, 'Sure son'. Everyone is son to me – from seven to seventy.

Rikki said, 'Do yourself a favour – buy a sleeping bag, bring a flask of tea and sandwiches to eat between shows and when the matinee is over go into your dressing room. Have your tea and eat your sandwiches, then, put out your dressing room lights, slip into your sleeping bag and have a nice nap between the shows. I laughed and thanked him, but afterwards I realised what damn good advice it was and decided to give it a try.

I told my dresser to waken me an hour before the second performance so that I would have time to shower and re-apply my make-up for the evening show.

After the next matinee I tried the sleeping bag trick for the first time. No joy, I couldn't sleep. I felt my body was rested though, and gradually got into the habit of having my lovely wee sleep, and I must say that from then on I had a lovely kip in the afternoon during every panto I appeared in thanks to the kind concern of my fellow performer Rikki Fulton. He was a thoughtful soul off-stage was Rikki.

After the matinee, when he knew I was in my dressing room between shows, he would knock on my door and shout, 'Could you go a wee plate of soup?' He knew Mary would kill for a wee bowl of soup! He would then pass in the soup in a flask and let me pour mine into my waiting bowl and we would both happily tuck into the homemade soup in our respective dressing rooms.

And while I remember, Greg Fisher also used to knock on the door with the same patter, 'Would you like a wee bowl of soup Mary?' Greg was a smashing cook and, of course, he didn't know that Rikki had already done the honours. It would have made a good sketch. The dressing room was like a bloody soup kitchen, plenty of time for eating, but not much time for sleeping.

Jack was out of the theatre like a whippet. Not for him the winding down. I think he made a bee-line for the bookies to see how his 'cuddies' got on. He always came breezing back into the theatre in great spirits. You could hear 'Hello China' long before you saw him. What a joy he was to work with, never any complaints.

I remember Jack and Rikki leaving the theatre together in Edinburgh to collect the car in which Jim Byres (the baddie) and I accompanied the boys on our way home to Glasgow. Now picture the scene. 'Nice Lady' with the autograph book at the stage door – Rikki and Jack signed the book.

The lady said, 'I saw you in Paisley, Rikki,' to which Rikki replied, 'I never played Paisley in my life.'

Nice lady – 'But I saw you there.'

Jack – 'Oh for God's sake, say you were in Paisley and we'll all get home.'

'No I've got to get this right. I was never in Paisley,' Rikki went on.

The poor woman must have been sorry she had ever mentioned Paisley, but Rikki was Rikki and we all had to wait until the matter was sorted out, end of story.

Rikki used to do all the driving in his own rather grand car from the King's Theatre, Edinburgh to Glasgow every night. He strolled up to get the car whilst Jack had a quick fag, and Jim Byres and I hit the chippie for a fish supper. We were always starving after the second show. We would quickly eat the fish supper in the street, but the smell would linger on our clothes and hands and not long into the journey Rikki would say, 'Have you been eating chips?' A chorus of 'no' us' could be heard, but we got the message.

Poor Jack had to suck peppermints to allay his craving for a ciggie. I can see Rikki now with his beautiful car, his beautiful fur collared coat and his driving gloves, every inch the country squire with his chip-loving, fag-loving passengers alongside and behind him. He liked driving, said it relaxed him, but many a good laugh we had on the to-ing and fro-ing from Edinburgh and Glasgow.

One particular incident which stands out in my mind during the run of the Babes in the Wood panto was the schoolroom scene where I was playing the stern school teacher to Tony Roper, Greg Fisher and Francie and Josie. I say Francie and Josie because no matter what the character they played it was always just Francie and Josie, or a disguised version if you like. As the stern school teacher, I had to say to Gregor Fisher,

'Stand up boy. Now, if you were out in a small boat with your mother and your sweetheart and the boat capsized, who would you save – your mother or your sweetheart?' And Gregor with that big lovable 'bawface' would say, 'Please Miss, I would save my mother'.

Teacher – 'Why would you save your mother, boy?'

Gregor – 'Well, Miss. You can get a sweetheart any day, but you can only have one mammy.'

The whole theatre loved Greg at that moment and it was Jack's favourite gag in the panto. I loved working with Gregor and Tony. The potential was there all these years ago.

Rikki didn't know what to make of me. It was our first panto together and he was to the letter of the script and Mary was just as the notion took her as long as it got the required laughs, but I was sensible enough not to do it with Francie and Josie. I knew better than that, but I did have some fun with the rest of the cast.

We had a handsome big King Dominic, chain mail and all my patter to him (not in the script, of course) was 'my, what a fine big man for a king, I wouldn't mind taking him home for a cup of tea and a fairy cake'. My mind was always on the next meal and Jim Byres (the baddie), who was doing an advert for Baxter's soup, got 'Come on Willie Baxter it's you and I for the Gourock bus'. It was all unscripted but the lads and I got a good laugh especially when I was in my comedy gear. I remember the late Jimmy Logan coming back stage and saying 'Mary, that's the best I've seen you play'. I was so chuffed.

Life as a professional entertainer and performer is very different to other jobs but one thing they have in common is that it's a mix of good bits and bad bits and as long as there more good bits then life is generally alright. But if there's more bad bits than good then it's time to get another job! Let me give you a flavour of some of the OFF stage antics which can help make the job such fun.

Jack and Rikki were sharing a dressing room opposite Tony and Gregor during the run, and one night when they were onstage doing their comedy spot as the robbers, Jack wandered in to their dressing room, saw some corn beef on a table and quite unconsciously picked up a slice, popped back to his dressing room, and had it on a buttered roll. He did this for three nights running – don't ask me why.

On the fourth night, Gregor said, 'Jack, there's somebody coming in to our dressing room and stealing our corn beef,' and Jack said words to the effect that surely nobody would do that? To which Gregor responded, 'We know they are, because we have the slices counted.'

Jack never let on that HE was the culprit, but he had been snitched on, so he was called 'the corn beef king' and everybody had a laugh about it from then on.

Well, we had a lovely season, and returned to Glasgow for a bit of a rest after our labour of love. One morning about two weeks later, Jack had notification that there was a registered envelope waiting for him at the Royal Mail Depot in Clarence Drive, not far from where we lived. Off he went to collect it and when he arrived home, he said that the chap at the depot had said, 'I don't like the look of this at all' as he handed over an envelope thick with grease. And, of course, when Jack got home and opened the parcel there were four slices of corn beef in it! Tony Roper had posted it, and there was a note inside which simply said, 'To the Corn Beef King.'

The following summer my daughter Diana, my pal Anna

Cowie and I drove down to a very expensive health farm, Henlow Grange. If we had gone in the same manner as some of the other well-heeled guests like the Duchess of Bedford, it would have cost a pretty penny, but we were offered accommodation in the house used for the beauticians' training which was much more reasonable. We had the same treatments, but not the same pampering as at Henlow Grange proper. AND we were three to a room – the three bears.

Well, for three days we had juice and nothing else.

On the fourth day I said to Diana, 'Do you fancy going into the next village and we'll have a lemon tea. We won't cheat.'

Off we went, and we didn't cheat. I went into Boots the chemist for something.

A fellow passed me, and gave me a wink. I thought, 'This diet is working' . . . and passed out on the floor! Diana was shouting, 'Oh, my mother, my mother.'

Someone gave me some medication, maybe a whiff of smelling salts, and I came round, but when we reported back to the health farm I said firmly to the nurse, 'We are eating tomorrow.'

We all waited for the lunchtime bell, ready to sprint to the dining room like something out of trap five. At long last it rang and our spinach with a poached egg on top went down like caviar.

We did lose a stone in weight and Henlow Grange is to be commended. I think every woman should treat herself to a visit to a health farm at least once in her lifetime, but the trick is, ladies, to go on your own. You'll get company there and will be able to retreat to your own little room to read or watch television. That's true peace, and the treatments are splendid and relaxing. When we got home Jack said he had never seen Diana and I looking so well. Poor Anna spent a fortune on extra treatments and still came out without losing a pound. But then she was always a big lady to begin with.

We holidayed in the Algarve that year and stayed over in London for a couple of days. On the flight home from London to Glasgow I sat beside a very familiar face, Mick Jagger, he of the Rolling Stones, at the height of his fame.

He was a mild, cultured man and a delightful travelling companion. As we got off the plane, the young girls were at the barricades, screaming for Mick. I felt sorry for the lad – he had no privacy whatever. Show business has a heavy price tag at times.

Christmas was just round the corner, and I was happy to be home for the holidays. We were doing the same show as we had done at the Edinburgh King's, so that was a labour of love to me . . . no script to learn. Whoopee!

It is lovely to be in panto at Christmas. It is the children's time, and they are so good to entertain. David Hodge was our Lord Provost that year and he had great fun being Wee Auntie Jessie, dressed in my props for a publicity stunt.

I next met David at the City Chambers. A group of VIPs was invited to meet Princess Margaret, and as Lord Provost, he was escorting her. Jack and I were standing at a door, minding our own business, when it opened – and there were David and the Princess.

He said, 'Ma'am, this is one of our best loved comics, Jack Milroy, and his wife, Mrs. Milroy.' Then David added, 'I should say she is very well known in her own right, as Mary Lee.'

The Princess said to me, 'Quite right! Always keep your own identity,' then smiled sweetly, and moved on.

I always remembered her advice, to be your own person.

I was in Princess Margaret's company twice after that, once at the King's Theatre in Glasgow after a charity show. The other occasion was when I did a cabaret with pianist Peggy O'Keefe and singer Peter Morrison for one of her charities. The Princess never once looked up at the stage while I was performing. It was very off putting, but such is life.

Perhaps she didn't enjoy my singing.

I have been privileged to meet all of Glasgow's Lord and Lady Provosts over the years and they all came to the pantomimes on opening night. The one I found I was most in tune with was our Lady Provost, Susan Baird, and her nice husband, George. Susan was so down to earth, I could have blethered to her for hours.

That second year of 'The Babes' was a happy one. No travelling, and sleeping in your own bed – what a luxury. I recall throwing a big party which went on till the early hours of the morning. I think everyone on the Glasgow showbiz scene was there, and the entire company of 'Babes in the Wood'. I had it catered and laid on a lavish spread, but I remember that Jack and Rikki disappeared into the kitchen for quite a while.

I discovered later that they had looked at the laid-on food and decided to make their own arrangements. So Jack rustled up egg and chips, which they both loved.

It was a good thing the party was only once a year. I must have had one more glass of wine than was good for me, because I slept with my contact lenses in. Ouch! They stuck to my eyes in the morning.

At 9am the caterers came to collect their dishes, and I had a matinee that day. I said to my good friend and dresser, Jean, 'Keep the lights out when we're not dressing. My eyes and my head are giving me laldy.'

But we made it and the show went on.

18

JACK'S HEART ATTACK

We had finished the second year of 'Babes in the Wood', and the following year, 1983-84, we played the King's Theatre in Edinburgh in 'Sleeping Beauty'.

Jan Wilson played her brilliant Witch and Jack and Rikki were at their best.

I played Nurse to Sleeping Beauty.

Jack was his usual bright self, ad-libbing his way throughout the show, and nicking out for a fish supper with the lassies between shows. Greater vitality had no man, and we waltzed along, thinking nothing more than a sore throat could ever befall us.

As usual, Rikki was doing the driving that year, so we were dropped off at our flat each night. It was a lot of travelling and working, but we honestly enjoyed it. And Jack's greatest joy was to make the supper while I had a wee look at the telly. The greatest sound in the world to me is, 'Mary, your supper's ready.'

No matter what's on the plate I'll compliment the cook – so long as I don't have to make the meal. I've never been a great cook because I have no interest in it. The microwave and Marks & Spencer's food hall were conceived especially for Mary.

Well, on this particular night, after a happy supper we

retired to bed. I awoke around 8am. No Jack. I honestly thought he had gone to the swimming baths. He loved an early swim.

But something made me toddle through to the kitchen and there was Jack, having his customary breakfast, five fags and three cups of tea. I noticed he was as white as a sheet. When I said, 'Are you all right Jack?' he replied, 'I've got this awful pain going up into my head and across my chest.'

So I laid him on the bed and phoned our doctor, who immediately sent for an ambulance to take Jack to the Western Infirmary, where a heart attack was diagnosed.

I went through that day in a daze.

I phoned Rikki, who had to go to Edinburgh and rehearse the understudies, both Jack's and my own, because nothing would have made me leave him. The show in Edinburgh went on, with dear Walter Carr taking Jack's place.

I was visiting Jack daily with my friend Eileen Matthews (her stage name was Eileen Keegan, a lady with a lovely voice). What I would have done without her at that particular time, I dare not think. She was like a rock to me.

I was living on my own for the first time in 30 years, and couldn't come to terms with coming home to an empty house without my beloved Jack to greet me. I was devastated.

After about a week I telephoned Eileen and said, 'I don't think I can drive to the hospital today, I've got such a pain in my side.'

So Eileen did the driving and we visited Jack as usual.

He was poorly, but not desperately ill. However, during the visit I began to feel worse and worse, and Eileen had me admitted to the surgical ward.

She then told me, 'Mary, your daughter had a bump in her car and is having stitches in her head.'

The Milroys were in the wars, and poor Eileen was left trying to see to us all at the same time!

Little Mary Lee, aged 14, singing with the Roy Fox Orchestra
at the Empire Theatre, Glasgow

Me and Jack Milroy
getting married in
Aberdeen

Jack and Mary – the entertainers – always the handsome showbiz couple!

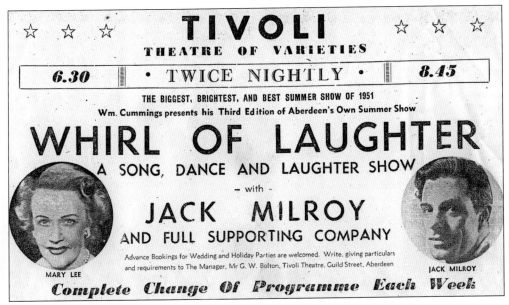

The 1951 Tivoli theatre production in Aberdeen – two shows a night
and a complete change of programme each week was a demanding schedule

Jack and me telling
our story to packed
houses at the Tron

The young Mary setting out on the road to stardom and, later, as Radio Clyde's inimitable Aunty Mary

Jack in his army gear, probably with taps on his boots!

Jack with Rikki Fulton as the legendary Francie & Josie

Panto time with Jack, Rikki and me appearing in Babes in the Wood

Another post-panto party, with Jack and me, Rikki and
Kate Fulton and our slightly less flamboyant guests

Jack accepting a lovely tribute with (left to right) Johnny Beattie,
Ann Fields, Paul Slater, Jack, Mary and the great Jimmy Logan

A proud moment at Buckingham Palace on 21 November 2000 when Jack received his MBE

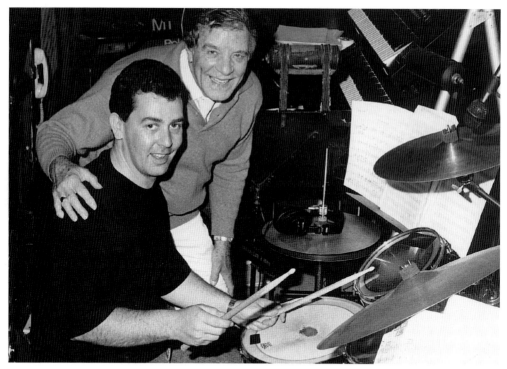

Jack with our son Jim, a talented musician

Life goes on – happy times again with (seated, from second left)
Diana, Adrian, Jim, Julie and friends.

My son was working in London, but keeping in constant touch by telephone. What a turn up for the books.

I was quite ill, but they were trying to resolve my troubles with a drip and a needle full of antibiotics. Jack hadn't a clue that I was in the hospital. They were telling him, 'Mary's got a cold and she doesn't want to bring her germs in to you.'

Our friends were doing double shifts with Jack.

On the Sunday night, Greg Fisher was just saying 'cheerio' to him when Jack said, 'Gregor, I've got that pain going up my head again, only worse.' Greg immediately summoned the doctor.

Jack's poor wee heart had burst and was slurping from side to side, back and forwards. It was make or break time. The surgeon came down to my ward to tell me he was going to operate on Jack, and to put me in the picture. I was lying in my night gown not sure of what was going on, unable to get out of my bed.

The family came up that night to me, and I heard myself say, 'Well, if anything happens to your daddy, we've had a wonderful life, so away you go home and don't worry.'

Poor Jack went under the knife and was desperately ill for some time. I was allowed to go into intensive care in my wee hospital gown and socks. Jack, with a ventilator down his throat, pointed to a pencil and paper and scribbled. What a job he had doing it. He wrote, 'Is this on the National Health?'

He thought I had admitted him as a private patient and cleaned him out financially!

I took the pencil from his hand and replied – no, I won't tell you what I replied on paper because it was very rude, but I still have the original envelope to this day. I told that story to great effect, making after dinner speeches, for years afterwards.

I discharged myself from hospital to go home and take up the strings there, assuring them I would return for a barium meal test later. All was well. I never did have the nature of my illness explained to me but it sure was a sore one. Maybe it was caused by shock. I'll never know.

Meanwhile, Jack was out of intensive care and in a wee room, and I was the only visitor allowed to see him for a fortnight. I used to go up every afternoon and Jack would hear the click of my high heels and know I was coming to his room. God help him, he used to keep half his cup of tea for me, with a saucer over it.

Some days he didn't have the energy to speak, and I would just read my paper to let him rest.

He gradually pulled round the bend, but by that time he had lost a good stone and a half in weight. When he was told he could go home, Jack asked the doctor to let him stay for a couple of weeks. This can happen when you are in hospital for a lengthy time. It's as if you become institutionalised and are reluctant to leave its safe womb, protected from the rigours of real life.

When I went to bring him home, Jack said, 'Oh no, you're not driving are you?'

I really didn't want to. It was nerve wracking for me, but the doctor had told me Jack couldn't drive for a year. So I thought we might as well start at the deep end.

Out we came, on a Saturday afternoon, me reassuring Jack that the football was safely in, and the roads quiet. We made it home, and the next few months were to be the hardest for Jack and I to live through in all our married life.

Jack's nature had always been outgoing and full of fun. But the operation he had, when the surgeon had to literally put Jack's heart together again, tends to change a person's personality and outlook, and he became very introverted and unwilling to see his pals. In point of fact the only person he enjoyed a visit from was the late Chic Murray.

Chic could be very understanding of illness, and he knew that Jack needed a quiet companion, with, of course, his comic genius coming out occasionally to make Jack laugh. Chic never outstayed his welcome and I would drive him home to his flat in the West End around 10pm. He visited often, and I am eternally grateful for that.

But time passes and one day I said to Jack, 'Come on, we're going down to Helensburgh for a blow of fresh air.' He got into the car with the usual patter resounding in my ears. 'You're going the wrong way.' And me saying, 'Quiet! I've been driving for years.'

Well, every sunny day after that I'd tap his shoulder.

'Oh God, not Helensburgh,' he'd say, no doubt thinking about my driving.

Then one day, sitting on the sea front, Jack looked across the road and saw William Hill, the bookmakers.

I said, 'Do you think you could make it?' Well he tottered over and put a bet on, and that was the real beginning of his road to recovery.

When Jack went over to 'meet the boys' and put a bet on in his latter years it was with my blessing, because it had been his turning point all those years ago. Within a year, Jack was back to square one, but he hadn't worked yet.

One day the phone rang, and it was his friend Ron Coburn inviting him to dip his toe in the water at the Gaiety Theatre in Ayr, in his spring show.

He said, 'Just you and Mary do fifteen minutes, Jack, and then toddle off home in the car.'

Well we did, and Jack was back.

Shortly after this, the Scottish branch of the Variety Club of Great Britain honoured us with a dinner in the Grosvenor Hotel in Glasgow. Both Diana and Jim attended, and Diana videotaped the speeches.

The top table was Una McLean, with Roy Boucher, the President and now ex-husband of Una, Anne and Sam Forrest, Lord Provost Bill Gray and his wife, Jack and myself, Kate and

Rikki Fulton, and Reo Stakis and his daughter.

We all made speeches. Una spoke for me, and quite beautifully I might add.

Rikki did the same for Jack, and of course Jack and I did some funnies together.

When I think of it now, the various speeches were a hoot. Una McLean called me the Maria Callas of Kinning Park reminiscing about my early singing days with the 'big bands'.

Then it was my turn to speak about Jack and myself. I remember saying, 'My Lords, Ladies, Gentlemen and Honoured guests. Isn't this a lovely tribute to this man and myself. I don't know who he is! I think it's an auld fellow I met at Butlins last year. But seriously, Jack and I have been married for the last thirty-eight years and it just seems like yesterday (and you know what a helluva day yesterday was). See if it was tomorrow I wouldn't go.' I continued, 'Marriage to Jack is like a fairy tale – Grimm. I said to mummy "are we having a white wedding?" She said, "Aye Mary, just pray for snow".

'Una was telling you I worked with the big bands. They were the great days. There I was the only girl amongst thirty men and too young to appreciate it. At that time I thought sex was the number before seven. Well, the time went by and I became fifty years old. I'd come out of showbiz to bring up my kids but when they left home I said to Jack, "I'm coming back to the business". "Ahh," he said, "who wants a fifty-year-old chanteuse?" but here I am and I sang 'Whispering', the Roy Fox signature tune. I said I was never too late for a cue in showbiz, just easily distracted at the side of the stage. If someone said to me there's a rare sale in Jenners I'd forget about my cue.'

Rikki reacted to this. When he got up to speak for Jack he said, 'I am shattered about Mary Lee saying that about never being late. I will never forget the moment when the witch came on for a scene in 'Sleeping Beauty', gave the cue, looked to her left, no sign of Mary Lee, so she went off (what would you do?). The cloth went up and a cloth came in and the pantomime went on, and the next thing I know here was Mary Lee up at me. I was doing one of my terribly quick changes and she said, "my God, she might have waited for me (sheer professionalism), that's your straight acting for you." She might have waited for me!'

He continued. 'Twenty five years ago last June, Jack and I came together in Five Past Eight and we've been working together on and off ever since and I'm just so pleased that he's looking so well.' He then said the last time we sat at a dinner like this it was very posh. 'It was the Saints and Sinners. Not that it wasn't great Reo Stakis, you done well. In fact, I saw him in the kitchen with his sleeves up at this particular Saints and Sinners do. We had a fillet de beef en croute which is succulent fillet of steak wrapped in exquisite puff pastry. I looked at Jack and there he was digging in with his fork and spoon. I said, "are you enjoying your meal china". He said "Christ, Rikki, that's the best bridie I've ever tasted".' Rikki continued, 'Over the years eating stuff has been a big part of our lives. Like the time we played at Dundee, stayed at the Angus Hotel and made the mistake of going into the bar. Big fat head in the morning. Went to a wee café thinking a wee bowl of soup would settle us. The waitress came up and said, "Oh, look who it is, which wan of yis is Francie?" "Please just bring us two bowls of soup and a kind word." She came back, walloped the two bowls of soup on the table and Jack said, "What about the kind word?" She said, "Don't eat the soup."'

Rikki said Jack introduced me to Chinese and Indian food. One evening we went to a Thai Chinese Restaurant and Rikki said I took fright and said 'I'll just have fish and chips'. They duly came. Rikki said, 'Jack, there's no salt and pepper.' The waiter went into his trouser pocket and picked a wee packet of salt out saying, 'You won sol?' He went into his other trouser pocket and said, 'You won pepper?' and brought out a wee packet of pepper. Jack said 'Thank God you didn't ask him for vinegar!'

Rikki also reminded Jack of an incident that happened in Dundee. Seemingly there was a wee man with a pet duck on a lead trying to get into the show. The box office lady said, 'You can't come into the show with a pet duck'. The wee man went away and stuck the duck down the front of his trousers and was allowed into the theatre. He sat beside two ladies who were eating their crisps. We don't know what happened. Maybe the duck wanted to see Francie and Josie, or maybe it smelled the crisps. Suddenly the duck's head came out of the man's trousers. One of the ladies said, 'Jessie, you'll never guess what's stickin' oot this man's trousers', to which her friend replied, 'Agnes, when you've seen one you've seen them all'. She said, 'you haven't seen one like this – this one's eating my crisps'. A Rikki Fulton gem to be sure.

The boys then did the Arbroath gag, a new version of it, which received a standing ovation. Then it was Jack's turn to speak. He was wonderful telling the folks about his army days, his start at the Queen's Theatre and marrying Mary the scunner.

He then said, 'When my act wasn't doing too well I used to sing a song to get out of the mire. Rikki has written me some crackers, but this one is for him. He hasn't heard it before.' He then went on to sing the following song with no piano, no nothing, just his magnetic personality. It went like this:

> Found a peanut
> Found a peanut
> Found a peanut last night
> Last night found a peanut
> Found a peanut last night
> It was rotten

JACK'S HEART ATTACK

It was rotten
It was rotten last night
Last night it was rotten
It was rotten last night
Ate it anyway
Ate it anyway

Ate it anyway last night
Last night ate it anyway
Ate it anyway last night
Gastric stomach
Gastric stomach
Gastric stomach last night
Last night gastric stomach
Gastric stomach last night
Went to the hospital
Went to the hospital
Went to the hospital last night
Last night went to the hospital
Went to the hospital last night
Operation, operation, operation last night
Last night operation
Operation last night
Didn't come oot of it
Didn't come oot of it
Didn't come oot of it last night
Last night didn't come oot of it

Didn't come oot of it last night
Went to heaven
Went to heaven
Went to heaven last night
Last night went to heaven
Went to heaven last night
Didn't fancy it
Didn't fancy it
Didn't fancy it last night
Last night didn't fancy it

Didn't fancy it last night
Went to the other place
Went to the other place
Went to the other place last night
Last night went to the other place
Went to the other place last night
Saw yis aw there
Saw yis aw there
Saw yis aw there last night
Last night saw yis aw there
Saw yis aw there last night

It had been a night to remember and the evening was enjoyed by everyone, especially Jack.

But it wasn't until I saw Diana's video the following day that I recognised the fragility of Jack's face and figure. He was healing all the time, though, so much so that when we were invited to do the Pavilion Theatre's pantomime as Ugly Sisters we happily accepted. It was a good show, featuring Dean Park, Stu Who? and Gwyneth Guthrie, Scottish Television's Mrs. Mack in 'Take The High Road.' Terry Lally, who was also in 'Take The High Road' at that time, played Cinderella.

Our friend Iain Gordon, the Pavilion manager, had the No.1 dressing room beautifully decorated. We had our own television and teasmaker and a lovely couch for us to take full advantage of. It was a pleasure to play a theatre we knew as well as the back of our hands.

After two years, Jack had finally returned to good health.

The heart scare had made him stop to smell the roses. He never smoked another cigarette, only had the odd spritzer on special occasions, and was tough as old boots.

So take heart if you happen to be reading this and recovering.

Jack's greatest asset was his outlook on life. Ever young, he didn't have birthdays. And I never heard him say to a soul, 'I had a heart operation.'

It's a wonderful way to live and an example to us all. He laughed his way through life and was a joy to be with.

Jack, Rikki Fulton and I did a 'King's High' show which was much enjoyed, produced and choreographed by the late Jamie Phillips and Dougie Squires respectively, the best in the business. And the dresses you got to wear were out of this world.

After this, we did lots of bits and bobs, and loads of charity work. I have never seen anyone so generous with his time as Jack and he never accepted a penny piece. A truly good man, Jack's stock remark was, 'How could I go into the bookies with my pals if I was special?'

But to me, Jack Milroy was very special indeed. There was not a jealous bone in Jack's body – I was always the insecure one. If someone telephoned Jack to do a show, the phone would hardly be down till I would hear myself say, 'Do they want me?'

At the back of my mind, and here I must be truthful, I've felt a little like Prince Philip all my life. You know, two steps behind, never sure if the promoters really wanted me, or if they were just pleasing Jack.

In the course of his lifetime, Jack had become a big star, and I was a well-known face, but certainly not in his league. How I wish I hadn't put myself through the wringer worrying about whether or not anyone really wanted me, because now I'm older and I hope wiser, I know with complete certainty that nobody in the business does that. If you are no longer wanted, they simply don't use you, and you then have to come to accept it. But I do wish I had realised much sooner. I could have saved Jack a lot of aggravation.

Before that day of recognition came, I had a lot to do with my life and enjoyed every moment of it. Jack and I had varied ploys. For instance, we had a go at the 'legit' theatre at the Tron in Glasgow, presenting a show called 'Nostalgia's Back'.

It was really our life story right from school days and we had fine backing from the Kevin Hughes Trio. We knew the show was interesting and we were professional enough to make it work. But, of course, the Tron attracts a different, younger audience, who were to my mind 'arty farty'. Would they appreciate our kind of humour? I was in a worse state than China before the curtain went up!

We had two hours to do. Just the two of us. No time to change in the dressing room, just a big rail of clothes at the side of the stage.

My friend Eileen Matthews, who knew the score, was kind enough to help me backstage. We couldn't have done it without her.

Well, we started. Funnily enough, the longer you're on stage, the easier it gets. And would you believe it, the young ones loved us. I did a nostalgic act and during the second half one lovely young fellow dressed in a white suit lifted me up in his arms and swung me round.

It was great. Jack and I got a standing ovation at the end of the show.

We played a week to full houses and left happy. Funnily enough, we didn't follow up on that success. We did it because we wanted to, but had no plans to tour it around.

The next time we hit the Tron was in a 'one-nighter' with Johnny Beattie, Jack and I, and a cast of thousands. The show was compered by Craig Ferguson, who has gone on to fame and fortune in movies and on American television. Way back then, his opening gag was, 'See backstage, you cannae move for false teeth and zimmers!'

Life is indeed odd and unpredictable.

Jack worked with Rikki Fulton on two more 'King's High' shows and to guarantee a sell-out all they had to do was put two names on the Glasgow poster – Francie and Josie.

Jack was at his happiest doing these shows but I wasn't

asked to do the following two 'King's High' productions. It didn't really bother me, but it did make the point that if they didn't want you they simply didn't ask you. And it really made me think. To be honest, I was getting a little tired of 'glamming up' for shows and was beginning to feel a bit like mutton dressed as lamb. Plus the fact that I had had a damn good run for my money.

'Mary, it's time to slow down,' I thought to myself. And indeed it was.

I could not foresee that the next three years would be busier, happier, and with Jack's blessing, a real success.

My new venture was to be the first thing I had done entirely on my own since becoming 'Milroy and Lee', or 'Jack Milroy's wife', or just 'Mary'.

19

'AUNTY MARY' IS BORN

Jack and I were doing a spot for STV's 'NB' arts programme, hosted by Brian Burnett and afterwards we got chatting. I said to him, 'I've got a demo tape of a radio show called The Aunty Mary Lee Show. Who should I contact about it?'

Brian very kindly told me to send it to Mike Riddoch, then the Head of Music at Radio Clyde. I did, and from then on, my life changed.

Why go into radio, do I hear you say? I don't know why other people do, but for me it was sheer bliss, the thought of going to Radio Clyde without make up, curlers in, covered with a scarf. In other words, it let me be my age and enjoy it.

I never in my wildest dreams thought it would take off. For me, it was supposed to be a gentle hobby. No more travelling, or 'eyes and teeth'.

The story went like this. Mike Riddoch and the station's director, Alex Dickson, listened to the tape, liked what they heard and invited me for an interview at Radio Clyde. They asked me questions like, 'Why do you want to do radio?'

I told them exactly what I've been telling you and I enjoyed the interview. Alex Dickson has the same kind of sense of humour as myself, and they made it very easy for me. The tape I sent in was 30 minutes long. They didn't promise anything, just asked me to do another 30 minutes, which I did.

It seemed to click. They offered me the Saturday night spot after the football. But it was two hours! So, back to the drawing board. I was so lucky to have had my early training with the big bands and lifelong stage work. My musical background set me up nicely. Picking out records was a labour of love to me, and telling all my tales of yesteryear and today was great fun.

The show was really 'a hing', a friend you could listen to if you were on your own, something the women could relate to, and the fellas were not averse to either.

A lifetime's experience went into the content, and radio is not an easy business to get into. You really must have something different to offer, or an approach to it that is primarily your own. Well, those are my thoughts, anyway.

But it was a medium which had a technical side which I had to learn. What support I had from Mike Riddoch. He was my mentor and sat in with me for about two months, giving me the benefit of his experience. He didn't change my programme, just made sure it was working as well as it could on radio. He taught me all the technical side a presenter must know and when he thought I was okay on my own, he left me to it.

I didn't 'drive' the show myself, something I have later regretted. But it wouldn't have been viable with all the chat I had to do. So I took in my box of tricks, records and CDs, and young David Tanner drove the show for me. What a joy the lad was to work with. He was clever, and used to slip me all the football gags. He was football daft and later moved on to Sky Television.

I cannot speak highly enough of the staff at Radio Clyde. Don't forget that radio is a young game, and I wasn't. So it is to their credit that they treated me exactly as they would their young presenters, with the exception of well-meaning commentators who would see me leaving my car and struggling in the door at Clyde and remark, 'Oh, come on, auld yin. I'll carry these bags for you.' Then we'd laugh together as friends.

My first programme was very exciting. Strangely enough, I took to radio like a duck to water. I loved it. Far better than stage work. At last I'd found my medium.

Jack really didn't know what I was up to, but when he heard my first broadcast he was delighted. From then on, his 'crack' to his pals was,

'She does it all herself, you know. I've nothing to do with it.'

With Jack's ability to make new friends, he was loved at Radio Clyde. He collected my fan mail. And what joy I had, getting feedback from my programme. I had regular listeners I knew as well as my own family, and I used to get a lot of letters from young fellows in the 'Bar L', Glasgow's infamous Barlinnie Prison.

Talk about being all shook up! Jack used to say to me, 'Aye, Mary, you've got a captive audience.'

Mike Riddoch told me how to deal with these, just mentioning the lad's name, so when they listened for their request the following week, all was well.

Jack used to say, 'Here's half a dozen from the pokey Mary.'

To be honest, 'Aunty Mary Lee' was very much myself. Well we all have two faces, one for the house, and another for dining out. To begin with, people used to call me 'that woman who comes on after the fitba'' but the show went from strength to strength. I didn't really know the power of radio until that time in my career.

I would go into shops and the lads would sing 'Aunty Mary had a Canary' – my theme song – at the top of their voices. I went to radio to hide, but ironically, I had more recognition from the public than I had ever had before in my professional life. Although it pleased me, even in my stage days I didn't like being recognised in the street. I found it hard to deal with.

Jack was the opposite. He talked to the world and his wife, and loved to be recognised. He was a joy to his public. I am a bit more reserved. But of course I liked the acclaim. Who wouldn't?

I introduced a character on my radio programme, my pal Aggie.

She was much loved. Most of my mail referred to Aggie, and regards were sent.

She was based on my very close friend the late Anna Cowie, who used to come on a Thursday night and play the piano for my daddy, singing the songs that reached my heart. We used to go up to town together, and she accompanied for Jack and me when we went out on our 'one nighters'.

Most of the stories I told about her were true.

She had a purse in her bag and used to say, 'See this wee purse, Mary? It's really lucky to me. It has never been empty since I got it.' And she genuinely put her hat down at a sale one day, and somebody bought it. She was good fun. Everybody knew Anna and liked her.

I had names for everybody, and nobody objected, because it was a fun thing and they played along. Johnny Mathis was 'Trembling Tam' and Peter Morrison was 'The White Tide Man' because he wore lovely white suits. Kenneth McKellar was my 'Ton Up Boy' because he ran about on his motor bike. Sinatra was 'Old Blue Eyes' of course and Sydney Devine was 'Steak and Kidney'. Ella Fitzgerald was 'Gie's Swanee, Ella' and Francie and Josie became 'Pinky and Perky.'

Jack's pals would say, 'You'll never guess what she called you Jack . . . Pinky and Perky. You'll need to talk to her.' And Jack would just go along with it and not mention that he had read the script.

Aggie and I always finished the show going up a close with a fish supper and a bottle of Vimto, or we'd go for a 'wee sensation'. People would say to Jack, in all earnestness, 'She and Aggie go for a wee sensation. She tells us, Jack.' And again Jack would remain deadpan.

The whole experience was just a joy to do.

I met so many interesting people down at Radio Clyde,

nipping in to do an interview. Russell Grant the astrologer was great fun, and all the pop groups came in. Great kids.

Jack and I had some lovely spin offs from Clyde. We worked together on two Hogmanay shows for television. The first was with Johnny Beattie, Ken McKellar, Gwyneth Guthrie, Carol Kidd, Katy Murphy, Elaine C. Smith and James McPherson, who was then one of the stars of Scottish Television's 'Taggart.' James is a good singer. I think he would have made a good pop singer if his star had shone another way.

The second year, the line up was John Grieve, Walter Carr, Allan Stewart, Andy Cameron, Eileen McCallum, Dean Park and Dorothy Paul . . . plus lots of bands. It was great fun doing a New Years' Eve show, and gave you the chance to meet up with your old pals. Mind you, when I looked at myself in the second recording I thought, 'Mary, you're looking tired.' But I battled on.

Wonders will never cease. Two years into the show, in 1991, I won the prestigious Sony Radio Award, announced from the London Hilton Hotel. It is, of course, an honour, and I was a very fortunate lady to receive it. A Sony award for just being yourself. It is on my wall and one of the kids will claim it for THEIR wall some day, have a laugh and say, 'Mind you, my mother was some stuff.'

So, two awards in my life, fifty years between them and never lost a sequin!

Radio Clyde 2 stalwart, the late Jimmy Mack, presented the award at a matinee show at the King's Theatre in Glasgow. It's the nearest I'll ever get to 'This Is Your Life'.

Many years ago Jack and I were guests on the Andy Stewart 'Life', presented by Eamonn Andrews. That was a magical night, which I'm keeping to myself, because it would spoil it for you if you knew the mechanics of it.

I deviate, and I don't often. Back to Aunty Mary Lee.

Two and a half years on, I was still doing the show and

knew I wanted a rest.

So I went to Alex Dickson and requested some time off. He was kindness itself, saying, 'Yes do, Mary, but come back to us when you're ready.' But I'm a funny soul. I go off on tangents, then I've had enough and I bow out.

After that summer, I truly didn't want to continue. I wanted to travel, and do the occasional show with Jack, and that's what I did. I've never regretted my decision to leave Radio Clyde, and I wouldn't have missed my time there for all the tea in China.

The station is 'The Best in the West' indeed.

20

THANKS FOR THE MEMORIES

Jack and I were appearing in pantomime with Dean Park and Stu Who? at the Glasgow Pavilion Theatre a few years ago when the telephone rang with an offer to take part in the BBC Scotland cult 'Rab C. Nesbitt' series. I was quite chuffed with myself. I thought, 'Sarah Bernhardt, move over.'

The young lady at the end of the telephone, always unfailingly polite, explained that I would play a housewife going shopping, and would I report to the BBC at 7.30am. Jack said, 'You'll never get up,' knowing how partial I am to my kip, but I did. I staggered down to the make-up lady and said, 'Don't make me too over the hill.'

But she insisted on removing all my make up and refused to let me keep my false eyelashes on, a real blow, as I never leave home without them – they're my trademark. The only thing I was allowed to retain was my contact lenses, and that's because she didn't know I wore them.

A head scarf was tied round my chin and a 'nice wee woman's' raincoat and flat shoes completed my outfit. I looked in the mirror and burst out laughing. I looked like Whistlers' Mother, only worse, but, thought I, 'This is an adventure, go with the flow.'

After a most welcome cup of coffee I set off with the rest of the cast on a bus provided by the BBC to go to the location.

And, my God, when I got there, it was the butchers shop in Allison Street run by my friends Anne and George.

The rain was literally lashing off the pavements, and there I was outside the shop, waiting to be called to do my party piece. In my scene, Rab showed me his tummy, vest lifted, saying, 'Do you want to buy a kidney, doll?' because he wanted money to buy a ticket for the World Cup.

I had to reply, 'Ach away ye go. I'm only here to buy ma mince.'

Gregor Fisher and I are old friends, and we had a good laugh. Success has not changed the boy.

After we had the scene safely 'in the can' I was sitting in a Range Rover outside the shop, when I saw the biggest pair of eyes looking in the window. It was my good friend Anna Cowie, whose nose had got the better of her! She joined me in the Range Rover, out of the rain, and laughed like a drain when she saw me.

The producer wanted a reaction shot of me in the butcher shop and Greg outside the door saying, 'Don't worry. There's always Paris, doll.' The shop was empty. They recognised Anna as a member of Equity, our showbiz union, and asked her to stand beside me.

I am grateful she came down that day, because our little contribution was put out on video and I can play it and see my friend, who is no longer with us. Viva Anna.

The episode went out shortly after, and I remember going in to work at the Pavilion, and the stage doorman saying, 'Mary, I didn't recognise you.' Thank God he didn't! That was my first and last straight acting part, but you've got to have a go at everything in this world. It makes life interesting, and I had a good laugh that day.

While it is in my mind, let me digress to a happy and interesting season Jack and I did at the Adam Smith Theatre in Kirkcaldy. We did a resident show for the first half and there was a spate of guest stars topping the bill for the second, a roll call of the famous of the time. The names included Bob Monkhouse, Harry Worth, Dickie Henderson, Sir Harry Secombe with a full orchestra, and Bernie Winters and his dog.

They were all great entertainers. And Jack and I had the joy of jumping into the car and heading off home to Glasgow after the first half ended.

The only two names that made me miss this considerable treat were Dickie Henderson and Bob Monkhouse. I always went out front to watch them in action. Dickie was clever and handsome, but it was sheer nostalgia that made me become a member of his audience.

When he was very young, he would go on tour with his father, who was a comic on the Roy Fox bills in the Thirties. Once or twice Dickie took 'Little Mary Lee' out to the pictures, as we called them then. I have to admit I had a teenager's crush on Dickie. I never reminded him in case he thought, 'My God, did I take that old trout out?' even though it had been so many years before. Men like to think they're eternally young!

Bob Monkhouse was a marvellous character, whose quick wit was legendary.

Bob arrived on the Monday to begin his week, accompanied by his wife Jackie, and visited with Jack and chatted for maybe ten minutes. He asked about the local football team, and everything that was news in Kirkcaldy. Half an hour later, he was doing his spot on the show with football gags, local interest gags, absolutely brilliant stuff.

I asked Jackie, 'Is Bob as sharp as that at home?' and she laughed. 'Mary, he can't even remember where he puts his glasses!'

Bob gave me a photograph of himself, on which he wrote, 'Why worry about life's energy problems when your smile can light up a theatre. My love to you, and my envy to Jack. Your fan Bob.'

That framed photograph hangs above my bed and has done for years. Bob had the gift of making you feel special, and I have never come across a nicer person or a more brilliant performer. His act was never the same two nights running.

Billy Connolly is one of my younger friends in the business. And yes, I hear you saying 'Mary likes everybody', but that's not so. There are quite a few I would like to give a kick up the eighties, but I probably shouldn't mention them.

I first met Billy when he visited backstage at some of the Pavilion shows starring Jack. Personally I didn't like it when I knew another professional was in the audience. Usually they sit very near the front (house seats are near the stage) and so your eye catches them while they are virtually looking up your nose, all very distracting.

But Billy was always different. He would warn the manager NOT to tell anyone he was out front and he would sit in the back circle and only surface at the end. That way he enjoyed a natural performance, without the performers being uptight because he was in. I don't always agree with his choice of swear words, but that's up to him. He is a unique character and a great performer. He sells out in days wherever he appears, and that's success in anyone's book.

On a personal note, when Jack was recovering from his first big heart operation, I was playing Dame in the pantomime at the Adam Smith Hall in Kirkcaldy. I really didn't know when Jack would be returning to work and thought I'd better get out and make some pennies.

During the matinee, my dresser came in and said, 'Mary, do you know that Billy Connolly is out front watching the show?'

Gosh, my knees turned to jelly. Imagine the Big Yin sitting watching me! He was doing a Highland tour, just him and his roadie, and saw my name on the bill and decided to catch the show.

At the end of the performance he came round to see me, to

ask about Jack's health and to see how I was doing.

I asked him, 'Where were you sitting Billy?'

He replied, 'I was with the lighting man in the back stalls.'

That was Billy. He always slipped quietly, unannounced, into a theatre. No fuss, just a kind visit.

As it pops into my head, Jack once told me a story about the late Diana Dors. He had been sent over to Belfast to top the bill, much loved by then in his 'Francie' guise. This was the very early days of all that, when his fame was really unbelievable.

I went over to Belfast when Jack was doing a 'Francie and Josie' special with Rikki at the Grove Theatre. Kate had come over to be with Rikki and after the show one night we stopped our taxi because we all fancied a fish supper . . . why not!

The lady serving us recognised the lads and said, 'Do you know what I'm going to tell you? You're the best thing that has happened since the pill and penicillin.'

They were loved in Ireland, and everywhere else, for that matter.

Anyway, the famous sex symbol of the Fifties, Diana Dors, shared the bill, along with Lynda Baron, who went on to play the plump nurse in television's 'Open All Hours' comedy series with Ronnie Barker.

Jack reported that Diana was quiet and unassuming, very different from her public persona in the press of the time. She would come to Jack's dressing room every night and say in her inimitable voice, 'Are they a nice audience tonight Jack?' and he would reply, 'They're just waiting for you, Diana.' She would then happily go and get her glamour on, with Jack's reassurance.

We met up with Lynda Baron years later when we went to see a show called 'Stepping out.' Also in the cast was a girl called Amanda Barrie, who had danced in many a 'Five Past Eight' show in Edinburgh. We all subsequently came to know her nationally as Alma, Mike Baldwin's ex in 'Coronation

Street.' I caught Amanda on a telly chat show and she demon-strated how she could still effortlessly kick her height.

You see, you never forget your early training. I still have muscles in my legs, with years of tap dancing.

Jimmy Logan was a life long friend. We both served on the Council of the Scottish Show Business Benevolent Fund. I'd take my bonnet off to Jimmy if I wore one. He always had great courage throughout any bad times in his life, and faced his final illness with immense dignity. During his eventful lifetime Jimmy did the lot, including flying his own aeroplane.

I once went up in it with him, and was as sick as a dog! I recall Jimmy arrived on my doorstep in Crookston years ago to ask if Jim, who was nine at the time, would like to go up for a trip in his plane, and invited me as well. Off we went, and I was never so glad to get back to terra firma.

I have no trouble with large aeroplanes but didn't cope well in a light aircraft, let's say. But it was a kind thought on Jimmy's part, and Jim had a fine day out.

Jimmy took his mum up for a flight one day and said, 'Mother, on the left you'll observe Ailsa Craig,' and SHE said, 'Just keep your eyes on the road, son.'

When we were living in London, Jimmy was appearing with Arthur Askey at the Palladium and we were invited to join his parents in the stalls on opening night. I noticed his mother was rather subdued, but just before the first half finale, Jimmy came out dressed in tartan and sang an appropriate song.

Then her loud voice rang out, 'Now you're talking, son!'

She was some character.

The year that the Royal Variety Show was on at the Palladium, we were keen to go and to see it, but the tickets were like gold dust. Then Jack registered the fact that Max Bygraves was on the bill. Well, as you'll recall, he had made the 'Bless 'Em All' film with Max when they were both just starting out on their careers. Jack popped round to the rehearsals to catch up with Max, who kindly arranged for us to be in the circle to watch the dress rehearsal. An audience is provided in the circle so the artists can get a reaction to their contributions. What transpired turned out to be a most interesting afternoon for me, observing first class producers being put through their paces. Because it was both rehearsal and band call, there were many stops and starts, but I didn't mind that one bit.

Norman Wisdom sang 'Don't Laugh at Me 'Cos I'm a Fool'. Max went through his paces, and Gracie Fields sang the National Anthem . . . another neat life circle for me, thinking back to when I was a girl, doing my impersonations of singers including Miss Fields.

In the end, I decided that on balance I preferred that we went to the dress rehearsal, which was more human and interesting.

Many years later I watched the first night of 'Barnum' at the Palladium, starring Michael Crawford. There were more celebrities in the audience than on the stage. After the show there was a fish and chips and champagne party in the circle and stalls bars, but we were not invited, not being with the 'in' crowd.

As we milled about and chatted after the show, a voice rang out, 'All ticket holders for the party come to both bars' and an usherette shouted to her friend up some stairs, 'Show these ordinary people out.'

When we reached the top of the stairs, the little Scottish usherette suddenly said, 'My God, it's Jack Milroy and Mary Lee. You're not ordinary people.' But we never did get asked to that party.

So much for stardom! I've feel like I've run about all my life catching my own tail.

It was in later years, when we both eased up a bit, that I appreciated time with my family, and Jack and I could enjoy regular visits to London to catch all the new shows. We would do the first nights and always stayed at the Regent Palace Hotel, not because it's perhaps a little less expensive, but because it is slap bang in the heart of London.

Jack was always extremely generous to us all. When the London Hilton was being built, he said, 'Mary, we are all going to spend a week there,' and he kept his word. I recall the trip with pleasure, the breakfast being brought in on a trolley by a flunkey, and everything on ice. What a delight.

Each day we would do the matinees. I went to see John Mortimer's play 'Journey Round My Father' with Sir Alec Guinness taking the father role. The heavily autobiographical story is about a blind QC and his relationship with his son. It was splendid and the last haunting speech was so sad. The father had died and the son was asked, 'How do you feel without your father?' and the curtain dropped on one word, 'Lonely.'

I left the theatre deeply affected by this beautiful play.

Outside I bought an evening paper from a newsstand. The date jumped out at me. It was the anniversary of my own father's death. It was as if he was saying to me, 'Did you forget, Mary?' He put such store on birthdays, sometimes even putting up his previous year's cards. All that gave him pleasure.

We went to plenty of first nights, but one of the most enjoyable for both of us was 'Mack and Mabel' at the Piccadilly, a story about the romance between G. W. Griffiths and Mabel Norma, of the silent movie era. It was wonderful and the music was terrific. Indeed, we loved it so much we went back the very next night to enjoy it all over again.

My favourite number from the show is 'I Won't Send Roses', a song I played many times when I was doing my Radio Clyde show.

Jack's absolute personal best, so to speak, was 'Chicago', which he adored. He especially loved the big 'Razzle Dazzle' production number, and solo, he comfortably beat our 'Mack and Mabel' two-in-a-row. I reckon he went to 'Chicago' six, maybe even seven times, just after it opened.

But it was to be a different American city where we'd spend many happy times over the years.

21

NEW YORK, NEW YORK!

After I left radio, Jack and I did quite a spate of work for a young Glasgow-based impresario called Robert C. Kelly. Very go-ahead, Robert is exceptionally clever and extremely kind. Many a comfy drive I've had in his beautiful car on my way to other peoples opening nights. Robert produced two seasons of 'Laughing Room Only', starring Jack, Walter Carr, Jimmy Logan and Johnny Beattie. Very successful they were, too, at the Pavilion Theatre in Glasgow.

When Robert and I meet, we often talk about New York, which reminds me that I never did tell you about my subsequent visits to America.

The second visit was to the Garden State Art Centre in New Jersey and we were there for one night. It's like an enormous Hollywood Bowl. The orchestra was flown in from Canada and Cy, our pianist, had only been Judy Garland's pianist! Boy, could he rummel the ivories.

The cast was Moira Anderson, Calum Kennedy, Jack and myself. It was rather intimidating, as there must have been around 5,000 people in the arena. Jack and I did a warm up spot and it was fine, because it was mostly Scots who had emigrated bringing their kids along to see their mum and dad's favourites from back home.

I could hear Jack announce me as I waited to do my solo

nostalgic spot and I walked on. It seemed like a marathon to the centre microphone. I started off with a standard, 'Cabaret' I think it was, then talked of my young days in the bands.

I said, 'Does anyone here remember Roy Fox?'

And a lady's voice from the front row shouted, 'Oh my God! It's Mary McDevitt!' Well, I was right at home after that, and loved every minute of it.

Moira Anderson was a good travelling companion, with a lively sense of humour and she did a lovely impression of the late Duncan McCrae. When we had finished at the Garden State Art Centre, we were going to have a couple of days sightseeing then make our way home to Scotland.

Ross Bowie, who had organised the tour, was travelling with us. (The late Ross Bowie was the father of Radio Clyde 2's George Bowie and was an entrepreneur and agent of note at the time.) He asked us to meet him at the coffee shop, and offered us a date in Atlantic City, to do the cabaret for a Scottish Society annual dinner. The line up was to be Calum Kennedy, Jack and myself. When I heard 'Atlantic City', my eyes lit up. I could hear 'Take me down to the Boardwalk' ringing in my ears, and accepted eagerly.

So we three, plus Ross, made our way to Atlantic City.

Well, what a let down!

It was a broken down holiday resort, with little going for it. I remember taking a photograph from my hotel bedroom window to show the folks back home.

But if I had bought some property there then for around £10,000 say, I would be a millionairess today. Atlantic City is now the gambling centre nearest to New York but in those days Americans had to fly to Las Vegas to gamble.

We did a show in a hotel on the Boardwalk. Now this was classy enough. We did a band call that seemed to take forever, with a jazz outfit.

Calum, Jack and I struggled, and won.

We got to the hotel in the evening and had bedrooms allocated to us to change in, kilts for the men, and me into my glamour stuff. No tartan sashes for Mary, no way. When we were dressed, we struggled through endless kitchens to reach the entrance to the stage. But when we got there, it was a sight to behold.

The men were splendid in their kilts, and their partners wore beautiful dresses. And the ladies on the committee wore white dresses with tartan sashes.

The three of us struggled through an hour and a half, hard going but the audience loved us. After the show we had dinner with the committee and left. But the lads were in the mood for making a night of it, so we walked along the Boardwalk. Jack fancied a paddle in the water.

Picture the scene, Mary Lee left on the Boardwalk to keep watch over the discarded socks and shoes. They came back an hour later!

We walked on, meeting up with two tartan-sashed ladies, who pointed us in the right direction for a dram, at Nell's Bar up the road.

When we arrived Jack and Calum still had their bare feet. Nell said, 'Now boys, you can't come in here without shoes and stockings,' gave them a towel, and we duly made the grade for entrance. Then the boys went their miles, especially Jack, who ended up ON Nell's bar, singing, 'If You Knew Susie' and tap dancing.

We left at 4.30am, got to bed at 5am, and Ross Bowie, who had been with us, don't forget, knocked on our bedroom door at 6am! Ross always got by on very little sleep but that was ridiculous.

Jack shouted, 'Is Calum up yet?' And when Ross said, 'No,' Jack said 'We'll get up when he does.' Eventually we had to drag Calum out of bed and it was a sleepy car journey all the way back to New York.

I hit the hay early that night, but the bold Jack hit Broadway once again. By 2.30am there was still no sign of Jack. By this time I had him 'laid out', was counting up the policies and was going generally demented.

Then he strolled in saying, 'Mary, you'll not believe this. There's topless dancers in every bar,' something we did not see at home at that time. I was just so glad to see him, he was immediately forgiven.

Our next American sojourn was different. I said to Jack, 'We always work when we are in the States. I would love a holiday, just to go where I please and relax.'

Boy did we enjoy ourselves.

I don't know whether it still stands, but then, the best way to go where you fancy Stateside was to fly to New York, then get the internal flights much cheaper.

We arrived in the Big Apple, and first things first, booked up some shows.

On our first evening we went to see 'Gypsy', the story of Gypsy Rose Lee, the famous stripper who was a lady to the end. Based on her true life story, it starred Angela Lansbury, with a very young Bonnie Langford as Gypsy as a kid.

There we were, dressed in our best, seated in the stalls and raring to go. Then I looked at the guy sitting next to me. He was wearing a ladies suit and hat and an old fashioned fox fur, and wait for it, was sporting a hefty beard and no make-up. I nodded politely. I've seen many a thing in my time, but this one took the biscuit.

The next night (we never missed a night when there was a show to be seen) was the Andrews Sisters in a musical. They were the most popular singing group in America in the 1940s and the show never came to Britain. There were only two of them, one having died some years earlier, and the whole show was based around finding a third 'sister' to make up the act. They danced up and down stairs and had support stockings to ease the pain. I've done the same many a time myself!

On our third night, we visited the famous Waldorf Astoria, to see Peggy Lee in cabaret. My good friend Anna Cowie had put me right, told me that they did two shows, and if you went to the second you could just go in, and if a table was available, have a drink, no need to pay for dinner. When we entered the beautiful Waldorf restaurant, we queued up then a waiter took us right to the back of the room.

I whispered to Jack, 'Tip him ten dollars.' Talking the universal language worked, and we were promptly moved stage front!

At last the legendary Peggy Lee made her entrance, looking wonderful. Beautifully dressed, she sang a batch of numbers I had never heard. I ached to hear her sing 'Is That All There Is?' and 'Fever' – all the old ones. Don't misunderstand me. She sang superbly, just not the numbers I wanted to hear and I was slightly disappointed, after being a fan for years.

Jack was not a big band or singer fan, with the exception of Frank Sinatra and Barry Manilow . . . but he would come along to keep me company. So I was really proud the year I arranged a present for Jack that I knew he really would like for Christmas.

Jack truthfully wanted nothing, had no time for material things, and was a hard person to buy a gift for. If I said, 'Would you like a nice sweater?' Jack would reply, 'I've got thousands of sweaters already,' when he had maybe three. The family all knew what he liked – stationery, razor blades and after shave lotion. Not very imaginative.

I can't tell you how many times I was sent back to shops with my tail between my legs with shirts, trousers, raincoats. You name it, I've returned it!

But Jack always stopped in his tracks when he heard 'Old Blue Eyes' on the radio so I decided to try for a signed photograph of Sinatra in time for Christmas, and wrote to his organisation that Jack was a much loved Scottish comedian and had been very ill. (This was soon after Jack's heart scare.)

'It would be a great personal favour to me,' I went on, 'if Frank could send a signed photo for Christmas.' Well, long time no hear, then three days before the big day, it arrived. I had it framed and wrapped up under the tree. The look on Jack's face when he received it was a joy to behold.

Running true to form on our New York trip, Jack found a friendly bookies and soon learned what 'win, place or show' meant! So I was free to do the city.

I took a cab to 42nd Street. I heard the song in my head, thought about the film and all the tapping chorus girls and decided to go there. When the cab dropped me off, I was in the centre of a street full of junkies and porn movies.

I'm a starer, and one fellow standing at the back of a chair which accommodated his lady, said, 'What the hell are you looking at, ma'am?' Well, my wee legs went like the clappers to grab a cab and get the hell out of there.

The next day was a trip to the top of the Empire State Building and lunch at a lovely restaurant called 'Top of the Sixes'.

Eventually, we were on our merry way again and it was 'Hollywood, here we come!' and we flew to Los Angeles. Our hotel was definitely 'Sunset Boulevard', with photographs of Mary Pickford on the walls.

We went for a walk and I couldn't understand much of the language. In short, we were in the Puerto Rican district. So we moved to the Beverly Hills Hotel and the magic began.

We stopped in at Grouman's Chinese Theatre to see all the hand prints of the stars in the famous forecourt and Jack took a photo of me against the stars' prints.

It wasn't till I came home and had my photos developed that I realized I was standing on the star of Victor McGlagen, who was my father's sergeant major in World War One! It was as if Wullie was saying to me, 'See Mary, I told you so.' That was my dad's greatest claim to fame.

One day we took a toddle to Santa Monica, a very exclusive area, and bumped into an old pal from Scotland, who was a member of a Scottish club there. He said, 'Come and have a night out, and give us a wee turn if you like.'

Well we did. They were noisy Scots, and entertaining them wasn't the easiest number. Jack did well, but they didn't want to know about me.

There had been a girl singing all night, so it was like taking coals to Newcastle. I thought, 'I'm dying here, think quickly.' So I stopped the band and announced, 'If you give me your attention now, at the finish of my set I'll take your addresses and write to your families when I get home and tell them I've seen you here tonight.'

Silence fell . . . my ploy had worked.

I did to the best of my ability write or telephone their folks, so you see, there's always a way out of the mire!

A month or so after we got home there was a knock on my door and a gentleman presented me with a box of book matches which had emblazoned on them, 'Mary Lee played at the Santa Monica Club.' He was charming, back home to visit his folks, and to deliver my nice surprise to me.

Our next port of call was Las Vegas, and I loved it there best of all.

Firstly, I loved the desert heat. I think it's the only time I ever sunbathed without breaking sweat, if you'll pardon the expression. We stayed in a motel called The Stardust, adjacent to the Stardust Hotel. We queued up in the corridor from motel to hotel, which housed at least 30 slot machines.

Jack's dollar breakfast usually cost him TEN dollars, but it was good fun. We dined on eggs over easy, hash browns, bacon and egg, toast and the obligatory coffee, and the waitress's farewell cry of 'Have a nice day.' Common sense tells you they are taught to say that, but it sends you away happy to begin your day.

I'd then get ready for my sojourn with the sun. Plastic grass, but so pretty. But not as gorgeous as the boys in their short shorts who brought out your sunbed and provided you with cool drinks to keep your thirst quenched.

Jack used to get on to the win, place or show, but always enquiring as to my wellbeing, saying, 'Are you all right Mary?' and my reply, always the same, 'Beat it, son. I'm doing all right.'

It was a running joke with us.

In the evenings we'd shower and change and go out to sample Las Vegas.

Dinner and a show, what wonderful, fun-packed nights.

When we saw the 'Folies Bergere' it goes without saying that Jack's eyes were like gobstoppers! The next night, it was the Wayne Newton Show. A Las Vegas version of Sydney Devine, he was a wonderful entertainer. They told me Vegas had made him a very rich man. Tom Jones and Engelbert Humperdinck were also appearing.

Circus Circus was just across from our motel. This was a casino and slot machines at ground level and an aerial circus going on above us. We kept looking at one of the marquees, with a caricature of a young lady with a big nose. Yes, it was the brilliant Bette Midler.

Jack wasn't too keen, but I was interested.

Don't forget, Miss Midler hadn't done any films then. At that time she was a cult figure. On she came. She sang, cracked jokes, some a little risque. She saw some blue rinsed matrons leaving, and said, 'Bye, girls,' and to her audience, 'They thought they were in to see Bette Davis.'

We had intended to stay in Vegas for a few days, but ended up staying for two weeks. It was pre plastic credit cards days, so we were ambling on with our dwindling travellers' cheques. Then, one night, we passed a small casino. Outside there was a pile of leaflets which offered you one pastrami on rye and a highball for free. It was a come on to gamble with them, of course.

We enjoyed our first sandwich and drink, and I said to Jack, 'Away out and grab a handful of those leaflets.' Well, the Milroys ate out on them for the last few days . . . great stuff.

At the airport as we set off, Jack put a silver dollar into a machine, and hit the jackpot – what excitement! We stayed in New York for another week on the strength of that win.

I loved Greenwich Village. I always had the feeling I'd bump into Barbara Streisand wearing one of her cooky suits.

I loved the kids playing basketball, and the arty shops.

I loved that more than New York shopping.

And I loved sitting reading my book on a bench in Central Park. One day, a little squirrel ran across the pavement as I sat, it was all so peaceful.

The kids roller skating, the old folk having a rest, the young lovers holding hands.

I'm a great people watcher, and a loner. I think most people who write are happy with their own company. I look at people and wonder what they do for a living, or try to guess. Don't misunderstand me, I love people and parties, but it has to be with people I like and can laugh with.

These days I can't be bothered entertaining though I'm selfish enough to enjoy other peoples' parties – 'We shall be home at nine o'clock tonight and hope you will be too!'

I enjoyed just wandering around the brownstone apartment buildings, looking at shops, exploring the theatrical district and picking up play bills to paste into my books.

And talking to people, I love that. I'll blether at the drop of a hat. Not as much as Jack but nor was I exactly shy. New Yorkers are usually too busy to stand and talk but the Scottish accent opens many a door.

Then, it was back to the hotel to my beloved Jack.

When I'd say, 'How did you get on today?' Jack would

inevitably reply, 'Not bad, Mary.' I settled for that. As long as he had spent a happy day.

We took a notion to return to the States in the summer of 1998, flew in to New York's John F. Kennedy airport and taxied to Manhattan. We stayed in a hotel right next door to the famous Algonquin, where Dorothy Parker held court with fellow writers such as Robert Benchley at their famous 'Round Table' gatherings there in the Thirties.

I viewed our room . . . no telly. In dismay, I called the Spanish maid and said, 'Where's the television?'

She pressed a button and hey presto, the wall slid away and it was ALL television! My holiday had begun. The month was June and I could hear 'I Like New York in June' ringing in my ears. But it was not so, it was the coldest June I've ever felt. New York – or was it us? – had changed.

First of all, we didn't drink, so that's as good as it gets.

We had a stroll round Times Square, the original laughter quarter . . . and what did we see? Bands of black evangelists belting out the 'Hallelujah Chorus' on every corner.

And Jack's pie fell . . . no bookies! Mayor Rudy Giuliani had really cleaned up the joint. You had to go to a race track miles away, or telephone your bookmaker. Jack commented, 'This is hellish Mary,' but struggled to master his withdrawal symptoms.

Sally, a friend who was living in Greenwich, Connecticut, came to visit us for the day and we took a cab to Macy's, the giant department store. We stood outside and Sally said, 'This is for tourists. This is not the real New York.'

So we grabbed a cab to Chinatown and the fun began. It was fascinating. I have never seen so many shops selling exotic fish in my life. No wonder you rarely see a fat Chinese person.

I bought a pair of lovely black trousers from a stall for two dollars and wish I had bought twenty pairs. They washed like a dream. I also acquired beautiful watches in Chinatown which turned green after a week. There are no free lunches in life.

But we did find a bookies for Jack. Chinatown was the only place you could put a bet on. We took him there but the cashiers didn't speak English, so Jack lost patience and didn't get a bet on. New York was well and truly in his bad books.

As ever, we did the rounds of the Broadway shows. Alan Cumming, the Scottish actor who has made his home in Hollywood, was knocking them for six that year in his first Broadway show 'Cabaret', playing the club's master of ceremonies, the role played by Joel Gray in the movie version. Seats for the show were like gold dust, but Alan organised tickets for us.

We also saw the stage version of 'Titanic'. Didn't fancy it much – we knew the boat sank. At the end of the week, we did something I had always wanted to do – we jumped on a Greyhound bus. And Jack brightening up now that we were on our way to Atlantic City, twenty years on from the memorable night he tap danced on Nell's bar.

It was a different ball game this trip. We settled in to a small hotel, Jack hit the fruit machines and I lost him for a week. He went with my blessing, but I have no time for gambling, it just never interested me.

I loved Atlantic City second time around, with its beautiful hotels and casinos, the famous Boardwalk where I sat watching the world go by . . . and WHAT a world. There was every possible nationality – talk about 'a quarter of dolly mixtures'. I have never seen so many fat folk in all my life, and I'm talking seriously OBESE.

But good luck to them, THEY didn't give a damn. The women wore shorts in the main, and you would have thought there were two wee boys fighting every time they moved their massive bums. I really went off my food in Atlantic City. People were eating like there is no tomorrow, and it kind of puts you off.

There were rickshaws with good-looking fellows pulling them, to hire to go the length of the Boardwalk.

There were not many star names at the main Casino. June is a bit early for that, not high season. But there were plenty of 'all singing all dancing' shows for the seniors who are bussed down from New York to have an overnight stay and gamble.

When we got back to New York it was pouring. It reminded me of Sauchiehall Street in Glasgow on a bad night, not something one wants to think about, really. I felt subconsciously we were missing Calum Kennedy and his great sense of fun, which we had enjoyed all those years before on tour. New York had definitely lost its charm for me on that final trip with Jack.

The city was so sanitised, better for the New Yorkers I guess, but I preferred the bawdy, cheeky city it used to be . . . and the terrible events of 9/11 were still in the future.

Back home, we settled in to a varied routine. We went to West Sound Radio in Ayr to appear on its Hogmanay party that New Year's Eve. Jack and I had finished our spot and made to leave the stage when the compere said casually, 'Hang on a minute.' Well, what a delight! Rikki Fulton came on to shake his old friend's hand and wish him 'Happy New Year'.

Both he and Jack were presented with a smashing caricature each from West Sound, penned by Malkie – Malcolm McCormack the cartoonist. It was a sort of informal lifetime achievement award if you like, and Jack was over the moon.

Early in the new year the telephone rang with an invitation for Jack to guest on Fred Macaulay's BBC Radio Scotland morning show . . . not bad for an 84-year-old.

He did so well, he was asked back on Fred's show again. He was a natural. Jack went in to the studio with his baseball cap on and the gags flowed freely. His humour touched all age groups.

As a couple, we did lots of charity concerts, and found them the best fun. Jack just loved people, and a chance to mingle.

Hogmanay that year found us doing a New Year's Eve spot for Radio Clyde from the Normandy Hotel for our old mate Ken Haynes of 'Ken's Ceilidh'. As always, John Carmichael's band provided the music. Jack loved it, and so did the punters. He spent two hours afterwards chatting to fans and signing autographs.

In the spring of 2000 Jack was back briefly at the Pavilion, the theatre he loved, being interviewed by an English television producer to give his thoughts and memories of the wee lassie he had featured in his pantomime 'The World of Widow Krankie' – Janette of The Krankies.

The interview was for a BBC television series called 'Fifteen Minutes of Fame'. Jack sat in the Pavilion stalls and I was seated a few rows behind him, and once again marvelled at his sharp and intelligent, funny brain. He never thought about what he would say, the stories just kept tumbling out. He praised Janette and her husband Ian. He was so proud of them and their rise to fame.

Working was easy for Jack. He was just a natural comic, which is a gift. You can't cultivate it, it's God given.

He always wore his lucky bunnet, a white cap he pinched in Majorca. It was just lying on a park bench. Nobody claimed it, so he took it home, washed it and it stuck to his head like glue. Jack always had a beautiful head of hair. HE said he kept it because he never washed it . . . as my pillow slips proved. And he always said, 'Have you ever seen a bald gypsy or Indian gentleman?'

He was always enthusiastic about amateur theatre, especially the Glasgow Apollo Players, of which we were both patrons. And of course, Jack had cut his theatre baby teeth in amateur theatre with the Glasgow Pantheon Club.

We went to see the Apollo Players' production of 'Oliver' at the King's Theatre not long after the news of Jack's impending honour from the Queen had been made public. During the interval Jack was presented with a beautiful little silver clock in Charles Rennie Mackintosh style, and two very special 'bunnets'. One is emblazoned, 'No.1 CHINA, MBE' and on the other is his popular catchphrase, 'SURE, JOSIE, SURE.'

When the show ended, its producer John Forsyth urged us both on stage, and as ever, Jack rose to the occasion, saying all the right things. Always the consummate professional.

22

BRIEF ENCOUNTERS WITH
THE GREAT AND THE GOOD

In 1989 we had a happy trip to London to collect Jack's framed front cover reproduction from the *Radio Times*, given to the personalities who had graced their front pages that year. It was a Francie and Josie photograph, a fitting tribute to two well loved performers who had captured the heart of Scottish show business for so many years, and it still hangs proudly in my sitting room. Jack collected two, one on behalf of Rikki, as he and Kate were on holiday at that time.

The presentation was held in the BBC London Television Centre, and though it didn't last for long – maybe two hours or so – it was one of the most interesting evenings I have spent. Others who received the honour that year included Sue Lawley, Pat St. Clement from EastEnders, Selina Scott, Sir Robin Day, Tony Robinson and Rowan Atkinson.

I nibbled my snacks and took stock of all the famous faces in the room. God, the women were so slim, I would reckon a size ten with the exception of Pat St. Clement, who looked as though she could enjoy her grub, but was pretty and beautifully dressed.

The only person I managed a brief chat with was Rowan 'Mr. Bean' Atkinson, who stood by himself and was easy to approach. I told him I had come down to London with Jack, and as I didn't know anyone else present was glad of his company.

He seemed to warm to me, and told me HE was painfully shy at these occasions. He wasn't a mingler. I doubt if he would even remember me, but I was much taken with this tall, angular man, who seemed ill at ease at show business get-togethers.

He's not alone in this respect. Many show business people are the same – introverted extroverts only shining when the show is on, but quiet people 'off'.

There are, of course, exceptions, people who are 'on' at all times. That is a great gift, and Jack had it. He was just as you saw him. He loved chatting to people he met on his daily travels round the shops, and having a wee fly bet on the side. He would come in the door of our apartment and you heard him long before you saw him, calling, 'You'll never guess who I met.'

The people who stopped Jack for a chat on the street left him feeling they had known him all their lives, I'm sure. A truly happy man, Jack was quite capable of looking after himself, very slightly eccentric, but all the more loveable for it.

And he always saw the best in everyone. I'm the opposite. I would say things like, 'Jack, she might have brought me a quarter of tea.' And Jack would say, 'Mary, if you got all the tea you wanted, you wouldn't be able to get in the bloody door for tea.' Then I'd laugh.

The year after our *Radio Times* trip, Jack and Rikki re-created their famous partnership for a show called 'Kings High' at the Glasgow King's Theatre. When they had previously appeared in 'Kings High' in 1986 and 1988, there were queues a mile long for the show. Marking their 1988 appearance, which was during the Glasgow Garden Festival celebrations, a video was released of their live performance, hilarious as ever. Would they be able to repeat all that?

Any worries that they might have faded in the interim in their public's mind were swiftly put to rest. Jack and Rikki were still the biggest draw in Scotland. 'Two comics together, still getting away with it!' as Jack was fond of remarking.

The show was staged with extravagant production values, beautifully dressed and produced. Standing out vividly in my memory is just one of the big production numbers. When the curtains parted, there were Rikki and Jack, silhouetted wearing the familiar blue and red suits, feet clad in thick soled 'brothel creepers' as their shoes were affectionately tagged, and of course, wearing the wigs.

They were joined for the song and dance number by the entire chorus, all the girls dressed either as Francie or Josie, exactly duplicating their costumes and the famous 'walk' . . . fantastic!

The restored Edinburgh Festival Theatre opened with considerable fanfare in the summer of 1994. Dating from Victorian times, it had been one of the famous Moss Empire theatre chain, now all splendidly renovated, with a massive new modern glass frontage. When the boys were booked to appear with the famous Tiller Girls in a special show, 'Francie and Josie's Christmas Cracker' that December, it was the same story, they were still a big draw.

But about five days before the opening an Edinburgh newspaper printed some remarks from one of the Edinburgh town councillors. He made comments along the lines of, 'what a way to treat this wonderful theatre, with a has-been variety act, two old performers past their sell-by date.'

When Rikki digested this, HE said words along the lines of, 'If I ever meet him I'm going to put one on his nose.' They opened, the show was a colossal success, and they packed out the theatre every night for its twelve night run.

One night, the manager alerted Jack to the fact that the aforementioned councillor had come along to see the show.

When Jack told Rikki, he went to town on the stage with remarks about him, and got roars of laughter because the audience knew about the councillor's comments, of course.

After the show the manager came to Jack's dressing room to say that the councillor would like to meet him and give him a box of chocolates and a bottle of champagne.

Typically Jack said, 'Sure, I don't care what he said about us.'

The councillor apologised for his comments and said it was the funniest show he had seen in a long while.

He had brought chocolates and champagne for Rikki, who agreed to graciously accept the gifts. In the end, they had their photograph taken together shaking hands. So there were no hard feelings and it actually all worked FOR the boys, because at the time of the newspaper article, people in the street were interviewed for the television news, saying they still loved them.

Jack was like me, not good at directions and finding his way to places. A few days before that show he was guiding Rikki, who was driving them, through to Edinburgh for rehearsals at the theatre, and confidently directed him up a one way street the wrong way.

They were stopped by two traffic cops who gave them a real ticking off and said they were liable to a £50 fine. Then one of them recognised Rikki and said, 'For God's sake, we've got Supercop here. It's Francie and Josie.' Rikki's Supercop was, of course, one of the memorable characters from his 'Scotch & Wry' BBC Scotland television series. In the end, not only did the real cops let them off, they stopped the traffic to let them drive across the street to the theatre. So you see, sometimes it pays in life to have a well-known face.

I was really knocked out with their NINETEENTH 'final farewell performance' at the King's Theatre in Glasgow in 1996, which proved to really be their last appearance together.

It became their last video, too, which has subsequently been released on CD and DVD.

Throughout his life, Jack didn't like spending money on himself, which was sad because he had to work hard for anything he got in life. But he really loved a bet, which I always presumed was a ploy to try to make money, but please! show me a poor bookie.

It was OUR money of course, but I did the spending, and I imagine Jack thought, 'As long as it's coming out of Mary's book, I've won a watch.'

If he had just finished a successful show with Rikki, a sizeable cheque would appear in my bank account. Always welcome, but for God's sake, you daren't ask him to buy a new blazer. Jack simply couldn't be bothered with clothes. I think it was years of dressing and undressing for the stage, and then when you don't have to, slipping on a pair of old jeans and jumper and his baseball cap was sheer bliss to him.

Rikki, of course, was the complete opposite, beautifully dressed, articulate, interested in all things that made life easier. Faxes, computers, you name it, Rikki had it.

Jack, on the other hand, wrote things down on wee bits of paper then lost them. But perhaps it was that different approach to life that made them so special together.

Jack had a wonderful brain, but was completely and totally lazy. But if there was something that must be done, it was done well.

He was deeply interested in what was going on in the world around him, and knowledgeable about most things. Jack loved nature programmes on the telly, and news and sport. Although he LOOKED as if he was just waffling through life, he had a sharp, acute intelligence.

Not like me. My mother used to say, 'See our Mary. When she looks at her most intelligent, she is thinking about precisely nothing.' A wise observation.

The nicest part of being a celebrity, or living with one, is the fact that you are invited to first nights and lovely shows. I get the biggest kick out of watching other people, old or young, performing, and one of my special nights was the Mickey Rooney show at the King's Theatre in Glasgow.

It's many a long year since I've felt such audience excitement in the theatre before curtain up. It was electric that night, and when the wee man came on I wanted to stand up and say, 'Thank you for all my lovely evenings at the cinema, watching you and Judy Garland, or "Boy's Town", or playing Puck in "A Midsummer's Night Dream" or the "Andy Hardy" films,' . . . the list is endless.

We all knew this was a one-off show, and savoured it to the last slice.

Our son Jim was drumming for Mickey that evening. Jim takes his musical ability from me, and like myself, loves big orchestras. A fine musician in his own right, Jim has handled being the son of Jack Milroy with great dignity, and it's no easy number in our business.

There was a party in the Green Room after the show. After about ten minutes, the great little man himself walked in and joined us. He was a wee, roly poly figure, but the old Mickey Rooney was well and truly there.

It's a funny thing, but since I've done so much radio, communicating with people on a large scale and yet feeling always it was one-to-one, I now feel utterly at ease with people from every walk of life. I found myself going up to the great man and saying, 'Thank you for a lovely evening, Mr. Rooney.'

He nodded politely. He must have been absolutely exhausted after his one man show.

I said, 'The main thing is, did you enjoy yourself?'

He said, 'It's been one of the most memorable visits of my life.'

It was a very strange evening for Jack, intensely nostalgic, recalling watching Rooney entertaining the troops during the war . . . odd how life comes full circle sometimes!

Another one for the memory book was when Jack and I went to a show at the King's Theatre in Glasgow to see Lily Savage in 'Prisoner, Cell Block H'.

I had bought his Christmas video and enjoyed it and at the interval we were having drinks in the Green Room – the King's staff are unfailingly gracious to the 'pros' as we are known. Pauline Murphy of the production team told us Paul had asked to meet us after the show. We weren't aware that Paul/Lily knew anything about us, but round we trotted to the stage door where we were met by his manager, who escorted us to his dressing room.

By now Lily Savage had gone, and a quiet, likeable lad stood before us. It seemed that in his early days, Paul O'Grady had played all around Scotland and was familiar with Francie and Josie. He had gone to one of their shows at the New Festival Theatre in Edinburgh. So he and Jack had a good old natter.

He worked so hard, and was so slender, I felt like taking him home for a plate of soup. Incidentally Paul sent me a lovely card for Christmas 2004, so he doesn't forget his friends.

When Jack and I were touring in our early days, most of the landladies had a book for you to sign after your stay. If you read it carefully, between the lines, when you saw comments like, 'Taste Ma's soup,' you knew it actually meant 'DON'T eat Ma's soup.'

It was code from one performer to another, and the land-ladies never twigged.

Ah, the famous visitor's book, and the Sunday lunch.

Never sure of when you would arrive, the meal was invariably cold meat and salad, and jelly and custard, not the most welcoming fare for a cold winter's day.

And the bed sheets were nearly always damp. I'm convinced

that's where I got my rheumatics from. Thank God I'm finished with all that!

But there were a few wee treasures we returned to again and again.

What I really hated was when a well cooked supper was served to you, then tantalisingly, the landlady would choose to hang around putting the world to rights, with you trying to be polite and inwardly thinking, 'I wish she'd get the hell out of here and let me get on with my meal.'

It was all part of touring life, and many a laugh we had.

These days are long gone, and most artists now live in hotels or flats, so progress has been made.

Getting back to opening nights, we went, again, to the King's Theatre in Glasgow to see the musical 'Cats.' Jack loved it, but his stock gag when asked if he did was, 'Too many cats'. After the show, we were piped down to the Hilton Hotel for supper, and to mix with the cast. It was a swinging evening and as we passed the producer Cameron McIntosh's table, Billy Differ, the then manager of the King's, introduced Jack, Johnny Beattie and myself to the great man.

It's a true saying, 'The bigger they are, the nicer they are.' I won't go into the outs and ins of it, but Johnny, Jack and I were members of the Council of the Scottish Show Business Benevolent Fund. Suffice to say, Mr. Cameron McIntosh is now a patron of our Fund, and proud indeed we are to have him as such.

As I recall Cameron McIntosh, I'm also reminded of the wonderful choreographer, Gillian Lynne. She is simply the best, and choreographed 'Cats' for him in so many countries. Definitely a force to be reckoned with, she has even been the subject of 'This is Your Life', and every dancer looks up to her with respect. But the Gillian I remember worked with Jack in the 'Five Past Eight' shows in Edinburgh as principal dancer.

One year, I took the children through during the school holidays and met her at various social functions, but my nicest memory is of Jack and I being invited to her flat. She whipped up a mean spaghetti, and a happy night was had by all.

No-one, I'm sure not even Gillian, could have imagined she would become famous world wide, although her performance was dazzling even then.

Another famous personality entered our lives, if only for one night.

Jack and Rikki were doing panto at the Pavilion Theatre. And at around 8 o'clock the telephone rang. It was Jack, 'Mary, get dressed and come down to the theatre. We're having supper with Sean Connery.'

He was with his then wife Diane Cilento, at the height of his fame as James Bond, and as unapproachable to people like me as an audience with God!

So – great excitement. What to wear was the first question and having solved that I got a taxi to the theatre, went into Jack's dressing room and awaited the great man.

Sean was watching the show with his wife and friend Jackie Stewart, the racing driver, now Sir Jackie, of course. The chorus girls were told who was out front watching them doing their stuff, and I believe they could hardly dance with the excitement of it.

We all went to an Indian restaurant, Shenaz, owned by a lovely gentleman called Lative, whom I had known since he was a young waiter. It was a happy meal but I was seated at the other end of the table from Sean. At the end of the meal, Sean, Jackie, Jack and Rikki had photographs taken with the entire staff. As we were making our way out of Shenaz, I finally had a chance to speak to him.

I said, 'Mr. Connery, I know your mother.'

Well, I got his undivided attention for the next ten minutes, as he told me he was really up in Scotland to pay her a visit.

I had met Mrs. Connery in Edinburgh. What a lovely woman, not beautiful, but with superb bone structure and lovely silver hair. We talked about what flowers to plant in her garden and I recall saying, 'Put roses in hen, they look after themselves.'

Sean obviously had a great love for her, and the wee chat about her made my night. Meeting Sean Connery didn't do my ego any harm, either.

And again, I still have that group photograph on my wall. I don't do it to impress. I just like looking at them for my own pleasure, and if any visitor picks up on them, I know they will get pleasure too.

Over the years, we became Aunty Mary and Uncle Jack to many younger professionals, like Ross King, who always looked to Jack as his role model, and followed him faithfully during his own climb to fame. In many ways, Ross is like the young Jack, loving his life in show business, and completely unspoiled.

Gerard Kelly also idolised Jack, and when he appears in the Glasgow King's pantomimes, always wears an old black wig that was Jack's for years. It's his talisman, Gerard's good luck charm.

Gerard also reminds me of Jack, and as he gets more mature, he even works more like Jack did on stage. He is a good friend, and very kind.

After Jack's heart attack, I worked in an Oxfam shop in Great Western Road in Glasgow. We were doing a fund raiser, and I telephoned Gerard, who was over at the BBC Scotland HQ filming for 'City Lights', the situation comedy series that brought him fame. I asked if he could do a publicity shoot for us, and he gladly brought over the entire cast. He had the place in stitches. We all wired into sausage rolls and cups of tea, and then back over they went to the BBC, which is a stone's throw from Great Western Road.

Good people, and Oxfam got a great picture in one of the newspapers, so mission accomplished.

23

BUCKINGHAM PALACE, HERE WE COME!

I was so happy to be out of show business, but Jack just had to be offered something and he'd be off, happy as Larry and looking forward to meeting his showbiz pals, like Johnny Beattie.

Mindful of his age, I would say, 'You don't need to do it, Jack.'

And he would reply, as he always did, 'Ach Mary, it's like taking sweeties aff a wean.' He just loved making people laugh.

Iain Gordon, the manager of the Pavilion, had realised that Jack was getting frail. When he booked him to appear in 'Not Another Hogmanay Party' in the autumn of 1999, Iain said, 'Just do ten minutes, Jack, and finish the bill.'

How Jack loved sharing a dressing room with Johnny Beattie.

Johnny said they could have written a book with all the stories they reminisced about, dug up from the old days. And they always left the theatre together after the show chorusing, 'The legends have just left the building.' They were truly great pals. Johnny always made Jack a wee cuppa tea when he came into the dressing room. They had their big box of assorted biscuits, tea bags and so on and Jack would say, 'We're self contained on the catering front.' And he would enthuse,

'Johnny looks after me, Mary.' He was very fond of him.

He did the same show, 'Not Another Hogmanay Party', the following year, from October 9th to the 21st, 2000 with me saying, 'You're not fit to do it, Jack.' But he had a will of iron and nothing could stop him.

He was his usual brilliantly funny self. What a tremendous spirit, and didn't he just love doing it, his pleasure at being at the 'Pav' again was almost palpable!

So now, in retrospect, I'm glad I gave him my blessing, because it would be the last time he would appear in public.

Jack's health had been failing in the year before he left us. He had regular check-ups at the Glasgow Western Infirmary every week, where he would be carefully monitored for heart failure. But if anyone asked him how he was, Jack always said, 'It's my knee that bothers me.' I never once heard him mention 'heart'. What a character. He was a joy to take care of.

We went up for our regular visit to the Western around September 2000, and his consultant said, 'Jack, I think you could do with the help of a pacemaker.'

We decided not to tell anybody. Jack wouldn't even let me tell the family, saying, 'Ach, don't worry them.' When this was done it seemed to improve the quality of his life for some time, so we thought all was well with our world. And it was.

We were sitting in the kitchen one morning, having a cuppa tea and a fairy cake, and the mail plopped through the door. I love letters, and made for the hall.

One letter stood out.

It was Jack's invitation from the Queen to become an MBE.

Of course I started crying.

Jack said, 'Why are you crying?' and all I could say was, 'Read this.'

He was very non-committal, but I could tell Jack was touched.

The letter was from 10 Downing Street.

Dear Sir,

The Prime Minister has asked me to inform you in strict confidence that he has it in mind on the occasion of the forthcoming Birthday Honours, to submit your name to the Queen with a recommendation that Her Majesty may be graciously pleased to approve that you be appointed a Member of the Order of the British Empire.

Before doing so, the Prime Minister would be glad to know that this would be agreeable to you. I should therefore be grateful if you complete the enclosed form and return it to me by return of post.

If you agree that your name should go forward and the Queen accepts the Prime Minister's recommendation, the announcement will be made in the New Year's Honours List. You will receive no further communication before the List is published.

I am Sir,
Your obedient servant,
William Chapman.

We were sworn to secrecy till the List appeared in print about a month later. Of course we told nobody, and when Jack's name appeared in the Queen's Birthday Honours, all hell broke loose!

The Press came to our apartment en masse and Jack was interviewed and photographed. I was so proud of him, as were his friends in show business.

Johnny Beattie treated us to a magnificent dinner at One Devonshire Gardens, the very ritzy Glasgow West End hotel which is a temporary home to the stars. We were joined for the meal by Angela and Jimmy Logan and Anne Field.

Johnny did us proud and I have super photographs of the occasion.

Jimmy Logan invited us to dinner at his home in Helensburgh and showed us his video of the day he received his OBE from the Queen. All in all, it was a happy time for us.

From the time one is honoured by the Queen, a good six

months elapses from the newspaper announcement to the actual Investiture. In the interim, Jack did his second 'Not Another Hogmanay Party' at the Pavilion and, as I said, he sparkled as usual, loved being on stage but was so frail it really worried me.

Just prior to his Investiture on November 21, 2000, we went up to the Western Infirmary for his usual Friday check-up, mindful of the fact that we were flying down to London on the Monday and that the Investiture itself was on the Tuesday morning.

During the check-up, the Professor said, 'I think we'll take you in for a few days, Jack, and sort you out.' He was dehydrated. What a predicament I was in . . . would Jack be able to go to London? Or must we cancel the hotel and flights?

But we were lucky.

On the Sunday evening, Jack got the okay to leave the hospital. That night, he was trying on kilts and all his rig out for the Palace, just as if nothing was amiss.

We caught the flight to London on the Monday morning, Jack using a wheelchair for the first time in his life.

The guy pushing him was so quick I was shouting, 'Wait for me.' I thought I had lost him.

We got to London, with a wheelchair again to the taxi, and on to the hotel, where we were met by our good friend Billy Differ, who had arranged a car, a beautiful Bentley I might add, plus a chauffeur, to take us to Buckingham Palace the next morning. Billy had also arranged seats that night for 'Fosse', the show based on the life of Bob Fosse, the great American choreographer and dancer. That was a treat we both enjoyed.

Billy was accompanying me to the Palace next morning as my guest. It was wonderful to have him there, and also to know that he understood Jack was not in good health. Billy did everything to make our stay happy, comfortable, and worry free.

The Big Day arrived.

Billy came to our hotel promptly at 10am to escort us to the Palace.

Jack looked so smart in his kilt and was really looking forward to the day. We entered the Palace gates. The driver parked. Then Jack, Billy and I climbed the long, red-carpeted staircase. Jack, being the recipient, was guided away from us, and Billy and I went to the visitors section.

There were three rows of seats on either side of the hall, slightly raised, so Billy decided we would sit there, and get a better view of the Queen than if we sat in the body of the kirk, so to speak, where you couldn't see for the ladies' big hats.

There was a lovely military band quietly playing show tunes and Billy and I sang along quietly but happily. Jack was one of the last to be honoured, so it was a nail-biting wait. Could he make it? And him with a bad leg, tae!

Eventually, there came a loud voice announcing, 'Mr. Jack Milroy, for services to Entertainment.'

Well, on he came, straight as a die, no sign of a bad leg. The fridge light had come on! He received his medal, and walked around to join the other recipients.

When it was all over Billy Differ and I joined Jack. I looked up at the splendid band that had been playing, and was now making ready to leave.

I shouted up, 'You did very well boys.'

The orchestra leader said, 'Thank you, Ma'am.'

Then an equerry joined us saying, 'They don't often get that.' We chatted, and told him we were lunching at the Ivy, which seemed to impress him highly.

I left to find the ladies' loo, which was miles away. The wee lady at the door smiled and I said, 'I couldn't live here love, too many stairs.'

I literally walked up four flights of stairs to arrive at the loo, and didn't fancy the walk back. I met up again with Jack and

Billy, and we proceeded to have photographs taken outside the Palace. Then I said, 'Is there no-one from STV or the BBC here?' and an Irish boy came up to me saying, 'Are you Mrs. Milroy? I've been looking for you. I'm from Meridian TV.'

Cutting a long story short, we were interviewed by the lad and they beamed it up for Scottish Television, where our good friend Angus Simpson, the newsreader, took over. Angus did a wonderful job of covering Jack's award and reviewing his career, which was shown on the STV news that night. Angus subsequently sent me a tape of the interview, which I treasure, as you can imagine.

Well, then the jolly threesome went off to the famous Ivy Restaurant and partook of a splendid lunch, Jack pointing out all the celebrities there and showing everyone his gong. He really was happy. He ordered sticky toffee pudding for dessert, and when it came to the table, the plate was adorned with 'Congratulations Jack Milroy, MBE' in chocolate sauce.

Billy and I lost Jack at the end of the meal. We sat patiently in the taxi, then Billy said, 'I think I'll go and find him, Mary.'

Jack was in the kitchen thanking the chef for his kindness, and giving him a wee tap dance. He had gone to the Palace in his kilt – and shoes complete with taps on. He really was a one off.

We got back to the hotel tired, but happy.

The next day, we went to see 'The King and I' at the London Palladium. Jack reminded me that we had seen the show forty-eight years before on our honeymoon, with Herbert Lom and Valerie Hobson in the lead roles. Talk about another neat full circle in life!

We really had a happy week in London and when we left to come home Jack once more subjected himself to wheelchair help. My daughter-in-law Julie, who is an air hostess, met us and drove us home. I think Jack was pleased that all the fuss was over.

He was glad to be home to his old routine, the bookies, his meal and his television, in that order. Quite a simple man, his greatest delight was jumping in the car, going to the shops and giving the people his patter. That was Jack in his element.

Our life over the Christmas celebrations was lovely.

Jack spent Christmas Day with his children and grandchildren, in my daughter Diana's home, and complimented her on her lovely dumpling, his favourite sweet.

He proudly showed them all his medal and I was sent home to get the tape of his Investiture, which was greatly enjoyed by all the family.

He caught all the Christmas pantomimes, including Gerard Kelly at the King's Theatre. Jack laughed with his pal Tony Roper, telling him he made 'a rerr Dame'.

He saw 'Treasure Island' at his favourite theatre, the Pavilion, and enjoyed it thoroughly. Always, I may add, with his friend Johnny Beattie by his side.

His last panto outing was to Motherwell, where we were treated to Anne Fields' hospitality at her lovely home, then on to see the show, with Johnny by his side as usual. After the show we went round to the Green Room, where Jack held court, with all the young professionals held spellbound with all his stories.

Jack's last professional date was with Robbie Shepherd in a show called 'The Reel Blend,' for BBC Radio Scotland. We had a lovely lunch at the BBC in Glasgow, then Jack recorded the show. As usual, he had complete command of the situation, and regaled everyone with his magic personality.

24

THE END IS NIGH

At the beginning of January 2001, I noticed that Jack was beginning to fail. When I said to him, 'Are you going over to the bookies' Jack?' he would say, 'Ach, I think I'll just watch the racing on the telly.'

I knew all was not well but we soldiered on, checking in to the Western Infirmary every Friday.

They kept him going splendidly.

Jack would give a sigh of relief saying, 'Thank God they didn't keep me in' because he was really happy in the flat living the quiet life, as he would have said, walking around in his stocking soles.

I noticed he slept a lot, but was by no means confined to bed. However one night, late in January, he had a bad night which, incidentally, was the only bad night he had ever had in his entire life.

I phoned his consultant and Jack was taken in to hospital. He went in quite happily because he knew the doctors and nurses and felt at home with them.

We all need friends at such a sad time, and boy did I have a good one!

My mother used to reflect that if you could put your hand up and say you had five good friends then you were damned lucky. My rock during this draining time was my good pal

Anna de Mascio, a fashion model for many years.

Anna really came up trumps for me. She ran me to the hospital every day, then fed and watered me in her beautiful home and drove me back to the hospital again.

One phone call was all it took, and she was there for me.

I sat with Jack for the last three nights of his life, and Anna sat with me. She would just sit quietly, reading a paper, her presence a comfort.

The night before Jack left us, at around 6am, I said, 'Anna, you'll have to go home and see to your own man, and the dogs.'

So, very reluctantly, she left me.

Tell me how many women would do what she did?

Jack died in my arms. It was on the morning of February the 1st, 2001, at 9am.

Weep not for Jack Milroy. He lived three lives in one lifetime, and enjoyed each one to the full. It was simply his time.

A wonderful life, wonderfully lived.

25

JACK'S FUNERAL

An intensely blue sky bathed the grounds of Clydebank Crematorium in brilliant, unseasonal sunshine on the afternoon of 7 February 2001. It was as if even Nature had decided to put on her very best show, the day Jack Milroy, one of Scotland's comedy legends, took his final leave.

Family, friends, and fans – 400 mourners in all – packed into the crematorium in Clydebank, just outside Glasgow. They rubbed shoulders with stars who had worked with Jack on the stage and small screen during his long career. All were united in genuine grief. This was not an insincere 'show business event' where the great and the good come to see and be seen. This congregation was present to say 'goodbye' to a much loved man and great entertainer, whose joy had been to make the people laugh.

They repaid him for the laughter and pleasure he gave them over so many years by turning out in such force to pay him their respects that people had to make their way upstairs to fill the pews, like an audience in a packed theatre spilling over into the 'gods'.

In death Jack had done it again – got a full house.

Clydebank Crematorium is set high on a hill with a splendid view of a majestic sweep of the River Clyde. It was Jack's choice. He told me some years ago that he wanted his funeral to be held there so he could 'have a grand view of the Clyde.'

Jack had also made it clear he wanted his funeral to be a true celebration of his life, and he got his wish. His fellow stars eulogized him, and the occasion was one of laughter and tears in joint measure.

I tried to be as dignified and in control of myself as possible when I arrived with my family, daughter Diana and her husband, and son Jim and his wife. We were also accompanied by friends of such long standing that they are like family – fellow comedian Johnny Beattie, singer and entertainer Anne Fields and Billy Differ, who became a firm friend of the Milroys during his years as front of house manager at the King's Theatre in Glasgow.

Jack's coffin was carried in to the strains of 'Ae Fond Kiss', an unbearably poignant love song in any circumstance, but guaranteed to make one cry in a crematorium. Johnny Beattie, the first to deliver his tribute to Jack, soon dispelled sadness and had them literally laughing in the aisles.

Johnny looked up at the balcony and said that Jack used to take a peek at the audience from behind the curtains and when he saw that the gallery was full, he knew it was going to be a good show. Johnny said Jack would have loved the fact that both the stalls and the gallery were packed for his funeral.

Johnny soon had the mourners chuckling with stories of Jack's life, including his recovery from heart surgery. He said, 'Jack told me they had replaced his heart with a wee heart, because less could go wrong with a wee heart. He was irrepressible.'

Johnny revealed Jack's decision not to have any birthdays after the age of 39. In deference to Jack's wishes, he added, Mary had made sure that 'Jack Milroy, aged 39' was engraved on his coffin. Johnny said his favourite story was the occasion when he, Jack and I had gone to the opening of the musical 'Cats'. When Johnny asked him his verdict on the show, Jack replied, 'excellent, but too many cats. It needed me and Rikki with a couple of Scottie dugs to break it up a bit.'

Next up was Billy Differ, who recounted how he had shepherded Jack and me through the ordeal and honour of visiting Buckingham Palace on 21 November 2000 when Jack received his MBE from the Queen for a lifetime of service to the entertainment industry.

Aware that Jack was in poor health, Billy had made arrangements to make our stay in London as smooth and easy as possible for us. Especially fond of Jack, Billy was near to tears as he recounted the day at the Palace, followed by the celebration lunch at the Ivy Restaurant. At that point, when he visibly broke down completely, I piped up from the family pew, 'Oh you're all right, son, you're all right.'

Gathering himself together, Billy managed to continue, ending by saying, 'It was a great run for a great man.'

Next to pay tribute was fellow comedian Jimmy Logan.

Jimmy, who was having chemotherapy treatment for inoperable cancer in his chest and liver, set aside his personal struggle that day. Indeed, he looked refreshed and healthy as he told the congregation that few people knew that Jack was a Desert Rat, who had fought in the Second World War.

Jimmy recalled, 'When I first met him, it was in the Queen's Theatre in Glasgow. Jack was just out of the Army, and wearing his uniform jacket, a kilt and a pair of tackety boots, but he still managed a tap dance to 'If You Knew Susie'.

In keeping with the spirit of the occasion, Jimmy ended on a joke, saying, 'I've been in my business for fifty years, and I never thought I'd end up being the warm up man for Rikki Fulton!'

Rikki gave the final moving eulogy.

The other half of the famous Francie and Josie double act which brought Jack and Rikki fame and fortune spanning several decades looked very frail.

He had been rushed to hospital after suddenly becoming ill at his home in Glasgow only days before the funeral. Kept in for tests, he had only returned home the previous day.

Like Jimmy before him, Rikki rose to the occasion, though slightly thrown by the fact that he had to read his notes using spectacles borrowed from Jimmy Logan. In the rush to get to the crematorium, Rikki had left his own at home.

Rikki said, 'Jack was a great friend, and I loved the man. I thought he would have gone on forever. There was this magic about him that will never be replaced. I'm determined he'll have a standing ovation today.'

Rikki was visibly moved when he said, 'I am saying farewell to my dearest friend. Working with Jack was a joy. When we were on stage I had no idea what he was going to do. Mind you, he didn't know what I was up to, either.'

And he broke down in tears when he said Jack was 'a true gentleman.'

Rikki sobbed as he added, 'All I can say is it has been great to know him,' and he walked away from the podium to applause from the moved congregation.

The fitting finale was when, in true show business fashion, the mourners rose to give Jack his standing ovation as the final curtain fell. Through their tears, they clapped and cheered as Francie and Josie's signature tune, 'So Long, It's Been Good To Know You' rang through the crematorium, which was far from sombre that afternoon.

There were smiles as the congregation left. It was just as Jack would have wanted, a truly theatrical send off.

My family, accompanied by Kate and Rikki Fulton, left the service as the Francie and Josie theme song rang out over the pews, to make our way to the Grosvenor Hotel in Glasgow for the post-funeral reception.

At the beginning of the service, the minister had announced that all who wished to should join the family afterwards and

I had decided, in discussion with the hotel staff, to cater for hundreds . . . and they didn't let me down.

Just about every name in Scotland's show business lexicon arrived to pay tribute to Jack. That day I tried to be the Mary that Jack knew and loved and I hope that I conducted myself with the sort of courage and humour that Jack would have admired. I was always so proud of Jack and I hope that on the day he was proud of me too.

26

REFLECTIONS ON LIFE FOUR YEARS ON

It is now 2005, and I can reflect back on the four years since I lost Jack, and it is the hardest of tasks to write about my time on my own, but I shall try to put it into perspective.

I remember the weeks and months after his death as a constant struggle to prove to everyone I could manage on my own, and I did succeed, but by God, it was difficult.

It was only then that I realized what the dear man had done for me . . . little things, like always bringing me tea in bed, being my alarm call bearing a cuppa on the mornings we had to be up early for a broadcast or rehearsal for a stage show, and doing small acts of kindness that money can't buy.

Yes, Jack was a good friend to William Hill on a daily basis, but always took his shopping list, to get anything I wanted from the nearby supermarket. Granted, I was writing my Radio Clyde scripts at the time, but his thoughtfulness made my task a damn sight easier.

And of course there was the practical side of our life together. Jack attended to all the bills and sorted out the financial side of our life, with the help of our good friend and lawyer Faith Cotter. I had to take up the reins myself. It made me stronger, but not necessarily happier. I was leading a different kind of life, dancing to a different tune, if you like.

Of course I had the help of my family, but they have their

own lives to lead, and I was determined not to lean too heavily, more for their sakes than mine.

I remember asking my friend Ella, mother of Billy Differ, 'What is it like to be a widow?' She smiled kindly and said, 'It's different, Mary.'

How different, I was soon to find out.

The first six months passed in a blur. I took the wise advice of my lawyer and made no major decisions about my lifestyle. I desperately tried to make my life meaningful, even went as far as presenting myself at church on a Sunday morning, but that didn't last long. There are too many gods for my liking, so I stick to my own beliefs and say my prayers in bed.

But overall, that first year wasn't all that bad. You can get used to anything given time. I was to receive much kindness from show business friends, especially dear Sheila Duffy and her husband, Paul Young. They gave me Sunday dinners and took me into the bosom of their family, and also included me in their party nights. Now that's religion in my book, say what you may.

Johnny Beattie, who was Jack's best friend, was a good friend to me, and still is. He calls me the Duchess of Kelvin Court and I call him the Earl of Huntly. He is a kind, decent man, whom I feel I could call upon in any situation.

Aye, you'll do for me, Johnny.

Johnny knows what I have been through. He had to find a new life without his beloved Kitty, and has made a remarkable job of his show business life. Johnny has one of the sharpest brains I know, never grumbles, and has such a sunny outlook on life.

During my first year on my own, I never turned an invitation down. My friends called me 'Mrs. Never In' but you have to get out there and find a life for yourself or become a very lonely, sad person, and Jack would never have wanted that for me . . . and do you know, every day makes you a little less vulnerable.

But as every widow knows, some days it's two steps forward, and four back. Which helps you realize that it's up to you what you make of the rest of your life.

I was lucky. I was able to work, so I said 'yes' to everything that came my way. I knew I was well past my sell-by date, but fortunately for me show business has a spot for the mature lady, and I grabbed the chance.

I went along one day to the Royal Concert Hall in Glasgow to hear the broadcaster and writer Clive James speak and was joined afterwards by the young chap who booked the personalities to appear on their 'Conversation Piece' lunchtime talk series. The names that come to the Concert Hall are usually flogging a new book, but Alan said to me, 'Mary, you could do this without a book, a talk about your life with Jack.'

So the seeds were sown. I was terrified of the task, but I knew I always rose to a challenge, so out came the pen and paper and the story wrote itself.

I decided I'd play a tape of myself singing with the Roy Fox band to alert people to my early start in show business. My good friend Lesley Hardie agreed to accompany me and do the introductions. A journalist, Lesley has encouraged and guided me through the writing of this book with great patience and good humour.

The talk was entitled 'Mary Lee – Jack and Me.'

I honestly didn't know if I could draw tuppence at the Concert Hall box office, and was delighted and frightened when Alan called me to say that I wasn't to appear in the smaller Strathclyde Suite, but was transferring to the main auditorium, which is enormous.

I didn't have the safety net of somebody interviewing me, it was just me, a podium and an hour long talk . . . quite daunting.

The Big Day dawned and I arrived at the Concert Hall to do a sound check and was then escorted to a beautiful dressing room. It had a sumptuous bathroom en suite, and in the sitting room stood a very grand grand piano.

A table in the window was already set out for a light lunch, to be eaten AFTER the talk, when the butterflies in the tummy had subsided. I changed into a pretty cocktail dress and waited at the side of the stage with my heart pounding. But once I heard my name being called I walked on and immediately felt at ease. The Concert Hall was packed with like-minded people and I felt it was such a tribute to my beloved Jack. Once more he had a full house.

All my chums had come out to support me, and to put the icing on the cake, Kate and Rikki Fulton were in the second row cheering me on.

The talk went down very well though I was glad when it was safely over . . . but you see, onwards and upwards, and one day at a time.

I was then invited to appear on a quiz show going out on BBC Radio Scotland, and what a joy that turned out to be. Billy Differ was our chairman. Maureen Beattie, Andy Gray and I were one team, playing against Johnny Beattie, Elaine C. Smith and Gerard Kelly. Well, we laughed our way through it. Show business is such a boon to the soul, and I was grateful for it.

Next I was asked to contribute to a television programme honouring Johnny Beattie's life and times in the theatre, and offered a part in 'Snoddy' with my old chum Gregor Fisher.

My social life was good, too during that first year. Anna de Mascio included me in all her social doings so although life without Jack would never be the same, it was interesting. I know no two people feel the same, but one thing certain to depress me was receiving sympathy cards. I also know everyone is well meaning, but hundreds of cards came pouring

189

through my letterbox, and it did re-open feelings I thought I had brought under control.

Four years on, I don't send sympathy cards.

That is just a little quirk of my own. Perhaps other recipients feel very differently. I think it was harder for me to adjust because Jack was such a public figure. God knows the general public meant well, but going through the supermarket was hard going. On any given outing I could be stopped by a dozen women. They didn't mention his name, just made remarks like, 'Oh Mary, he was such a nice man.' I felt at times that I was consoling them.

But time passes, and life has become a bit more straight-forward for me now that my late husband is a legend.

Anyone with any sense knows that health is number one in the scheme of things. I didn't, not until I nearly lost mine. I went on holiday with a girlfriend to Turkey, my first trip abroad without Jack saying, 'You don't need all that stuff you're packing.'

It was panic stations for me, but I did it.

We had the most wonderful week, lovely sunshine, good companions, lots of laughs, and truthfully I could have signed on for another two weeks. The Turks were so kind and it was my first visit. It was paradise for a week but the night flight home was horrendous, packed to the gunnels, and stuffy. I couldn't breathe properly, as if you were taking in recycled air.

When I got home I went to bed and slept the sleep of the just, only to awaken with no voice.

Let me make that clear.

It wasn't a hoarse voice, it was NO voice and it was very frightening.

And to compound it, everything I ate went down one way, and up the other immediately – instant regurgitation . . . MOST unpleasant. So I presented myself at the Accident and Emergency at my nearest hospital. My housekeeper Christine and I were there by around ten in the morning, still waiting at well after noon, but eventually I was seen and a very kind nurse told me I was being admitted. Panic stations! No toiletry bag, no nothing. All I had of my own were my false eyelashes.

Christine was so kind, and stayed with me till I was tucked up in a four bedded bay. She informed my family, who all appeared that evening, wondering what was going on. The hospital did every kind of test on me and the very last one showed vocal cords not working properly, the death knell to a singer.

I was to have gone home, but then a throat specialist came to check me out and decided that I should be transferred from the Western Infirmary to Gartnavel Hospital. So it was a ride in an ambulance for me, and into another four bedded bay.

Everyone in that room had cancer of the throat. I was lucky, and was sent home to recuperate, with instructions to attend a voice clinic. The throat specialist there gave me exercises to do to help bring back my voice. Christmas was nearly upon us and I felt okay, just unable to make myself heard, a boon for my family and friends . . . Mary had never been so quiet!

To use over Christmas my kind and thoughtful specialist gave me a microphone with a little amplifying box attached, so it was 'have box, will travel' for me. I went to all the parties with my little mike and box. It was AWFUL, but you don't have far to look for someone worse off than yourself. I felt like the lady with the heavy smoking problem in Karen Dunbar's television sketch!

I attended the clinic for a long time and did my exercises dutifully, but only one half of my vocal chords still worked. Nobody was able to tell me what was wrong, or why I should be saddled with this problem. The specialist thought I had caught a virus on the plane back from Turkey, but she couldn't be sure.

I would ask, 'when am I going to get my voice back?' and she just couldn't give me an answer.

Just a few months back, I presented myself to my throat consultant as requested and she viewed my throat again and said, 'the other side is beginning to work so I don't want to see you again.' I danced out of the door, told my friend Eileen Matthews the good news, and we went off to the hospital canteen and celebrated with a cuppa tea and a fairy cake.

What a lucky escape. I now have ninety per cent of my voice back, with very little singing voice, but dear God, I say again, was I lucky! I didn't say much about the fears that preyed on my mind, but all along I thought they would tell me it was cancer. I was so relieved to hear that I had the all clear.

I hate not being able to sing, you know, just for my own pleasure, but I am happy to be well. It was just one of those mysterious things you get. Personally, I am inclined to put it all down to the shock of Jack's death, some sort of dramatic, delayed reaction. But I'll never be completely sure.

27

FLYING SOLO

I well remember my first trip to London after Jack died. I felt so alone. Jack had done everything for me travel-wise and honestly I was very nervous about going away entirely on my own.

I sat in the train beside a little old nun, who was so sweet and positive that she gave me courage. I vividly remember thinking that if all she had had for company was God, then I should be ashamed to feel so intimidated.

She shared her sandwich with me, saying, 'Daughter, I leave it in God's hands.' What strength. She was like a little sparrow. She was met by another nun at Euston station and fluttered out of my life, but she did impress me.

I have a very good friend, a Scot who lives in London now. Tommy Lees is an accordionist who had worked the Scottish circuit. Jack and I always stayed with him in London and he with us in Glasgow.

When I arrived at Euston it was worth a million pounds to see his big familiar face waiting to take my bags. Since that trip I always stay with Tom in the Big Smoke. He just gives me a front door key and lets me come and go as I please, and it's such a comfort to come in at night to someone and have a friendly natter about how the day has gone.

We argue like mad, but always finish up laughing.

That first solo trip gave me confidence, and now there's no stopping me.

I have been away twice to Weston-super-Mare with members of the Scottish Music Hall and Variety Theatre Society on their annual outing in the early summer.

I am in awe of the spirit of the wonderful week of fun they lay on for us. We fly to Bristol, taxi into Weston, then it begins. Our last stay afforded us a packed programme, as ever. The highlights were the Ken Dodd show, the Joe Pasquale show, Old Tyme Music Hall and a beautiful ball on the Friday, before flying back to Glasgow on the Saturday. The evening of the ball was rich in nostalgia and hosted by Roy Hudd, the President of the Water Rats.

At one point he introduced Sir Norman Wisdom, who was presiding over his table of friends. Prior to this we had been entertained by a wonderful brass band, and Roy Hudd persuaded Norman to sing 'Don't Laugh at Me 'Cos I'm a Fool' with the band and I realised I was part of something very special. Wisdom received a standing ovation, well deserved I might add, and I found myself shedding a quiet tear remembering how everyone used to say that Norman and Jack looked very alike when they were young men. We also had the pleasure of seeing the Beverley Sisters, who belie the years, still looking great and singing well.

Jimmy Perry, co-creator with David Croft of 'Dad's Army' and 'It Ain't Half Hot, Mum', was there. What a heritage to leave to the great British public, eh?

Jimmy had written a book about his life, and meeting him was again very nostalgic for me. You see, Jack always loved to watch 'It Ain't Half Hot, Mum', which was about a British Army concert party in India during the Second World War, of course.

Jack thought the series was brilliantly done and so authentically detailed. When he was with the Black Watch in India, THEY had a punka wallah who pulled a rope on a big piece of matting with his toe to keep the verandah cool . . . a detail that Croft and Perry had written in to the television series.

I found Jimmy Perry a charming person, who incidentally did a very good act. I bought his book and asked him to sign it, and just as I was doing that, the man next to him said, 'It's Mary McDevitt, is it not?'

It was folk singer and musician Chas McDevitt, who was King Rat that year, 2004. Life is full of coincidence. Chas had been trying to get in touch with me to get some details about my career. I also met my old friend Jimmy Kennedy, who was the overall booker for Pontins holiday camps for several years . . . small worlds, and all that!

I tell you these details because whether you feel like it or not, it is so beneficial to join all sorts of things and meet all sorts of people.

The Scottish Music Hall Society is great fun. We go on bus runs and have annual luncheons in Glasgow and Edinburgh. Johnny Beattie is our President, and is very generous with his time. Show business is a great fraternity. It certainly keeps ME going!

Iain Gordon of the Glasgow Pavilion always sends me opening night tickets for his shows, and likewise my good friends Pauline Murphy and Yvonne Eliott of the King's Theatre team, who send me lovely invitations to their first nights and include me in the after show parties, where I meet many of my chums.

I have a friend who has a very bright outlook on life. She always says, 'Mary, grab the moment,' and how right she is.

Between all this busy to-ing and fro-ing, I took time out to have a hip replacement, which was very successful, only one leg is now a mite shorter than the other. But nobody's perfect, and I still wear my high heels, wobbly pins or not!

Nobody's life is all beer and skittles.

Annie Ross, sister of the late Jimmy Logan, came to lunch

with Angela, Jimmy's widow and she made a very funny remark which I shall pass on to you.

'Honey,' she said, 'age is just a number, and mine is exdirectory.'

I have dined out on that one a few times, I can tell you.

She asked politely during lunch, 'Do you mind if I smoke, Mary?' and I said, 'I don't mind if you set yourself on fire.' We enjoy the banter.

Annie and I put on our glad rags and made for the Glasgow Thistle Hotel to attend the Show Business Benevolent Fund dance. I've been on the committee for the past fifteen years, and Jack was their President for a couple of years. The committee is rich with names . . . Peter Morrison, Dean Park (our President), Alastair Gillies, Ann Fields, Anna and Robert Hewitt, Helen Randell, Peter de Rance, Angela Logan . . . and many more.

We do our best to look after the people who need looking after, that is our aim, and the ball is the annual fund raiser.

There is always the obligatory raffle and auction.

This year, 2005, I put up for auction a bunnet that belonged to my late husband, with one of Jack's famous catchphrases imprinted on it . . . 'Sure, Josie, Sure.'

His old friend Johnny Beattie modelled it, and to my utter delight it raised £1,000 for the fund. It was bought by the generous Ken Christie, sales manager with Singapore Airlines in Scotland, who said he was going to have it framed. So you could say it went to one of the 'chinas'. Jack would have been so pleased, and it is lovely for me to reflect on how kindly he is remembered.

This year's ball was really a splendid catching up of old friends. It was good to see the Alexander Brothers again, looking amazingly unchanged, with their lovely wives Betty and Lill.

Everybody was congratulating them on their MBEs, to be

received shortly from the Queen, and high time too, I say. These two men have brought such joy to emigrants all over the world, truly ambassadors of Scotland.

I was heartened to see Jimmy Mack's widow there. She attended with her daughter. A gutsy wee woman is Barbara. It is her first year on her own, and I wish I could make it better for her, but she'll get there, never fear. Jimmy, her late husband, was my colleague on Radio Clyde, truly one of nature's gentlemen.

And would you believe, Maidie Dickson, widow of the great Chic Murray, was also present, looking good, and Gwyneth Guthrie and her charming husband.

I miss her on 'The High Road', Gwyneth and all the cast, if the truth be told. Why can't they have 'The High Road' on Scottish Television and 'River City' on BBC Scotland, competing like 'Coronation Street' and 'EastEnders'?

Dean Park hosted the evening, calling my group 'the Aunty Mary Lee table.'

I must say my daughter Diana was beautiful and graced my table with her husband Morgan. I got up to dance, and was happily surprised to find I could still cut a mean figure on the floor . . . and me with a bad leg, tae!

Billy Differ was there with his party. His mother and I have much in common, having had our hips done at the same time . . . hip, hip, hooray!

We exchanged glances as we both hit the dance floor. Could we make it? You bet. Well done Ella.

As always, my table companions were my dearest friends Eileen and Gordon Matthews. Ann Fields was looking glamorous. We all scrub up well. Ann has done so much for the fund over many years with her can collections after shows at all the Glasgow theatres and we are eternally grateful for her labours.

She was there with her sister Sally Logan and brother-in-law

Joe Gordon of the famous Joe Gordon Folk Four. Sally and Joe always make an elegant couple. My friend Carmen Capaldi was in my party. She is another conscientious committee member. Myra Crighton, also a member of the committee, looked very pretty. She had the Crighton Model Agency in Glasgow for years.

It was a really happy night.

The cabaret was the Tara Dancers, lovely little children doing impossibly tricky Irish dancing, and bringing the house down. And thereby hangs a tale.

When I was very young, doing my impressions of Chevalier and Gracie Fields, a gentleman came to my mother's door and enquired if her daughter could provide the cabaret for the forthcoming Show Business Benevolent Fund Ball.

I don't recall doing it, but I must have done. Not so long ago I came across an old programme from the Playhouse Cinema, which used to be opposite the Pavilion Theatre.

It read, 'Cabaret by Mary McDevitt' and in brackets, 'wonder impressions'.

I would be about twelve then, and little did I know how much the same charity would mean to me in my later years. Life is a constant surprise.

And talk about being really surprised, I was going through some of Jack's papers the other day and lo and behold, there was a Western Union cable from Jerry Lewis to Jack, asking him to help in the fight against muscular dystrophy from the Scottish show business angle. How Jack must have treasured that, because the great American funny man was one of his idols, and he used to do a great impression of Lewis. Jack never showed me the telegram. Perhaps it was just too big a thrill, and not to be shared.

When I look back on the life Jack and I shared on the stage, I love to remember his classic sketches.

Jack and Glen Michael spent years perfecting material like

'The Scot in London'. Glen played the spiv out to con Jack, who cried every time his money was parted from him.

Another brilliant favourite was the butler sketch. Jack started off dressed in formal tails, began mixing drinks for a house party, and ended up totally drunk. It was very visual, great fun to do, and all ages could enjoy it.

They had a sure-fire way of raising a huge laugh when they felt a sketch needed a lift. Glen often played old characters, complete with walking stick.

If things were flagging, Jack would hiss, 'three seconds . . . the stick,' then kick it away from Glen and down he would crash. It never failed.

Another favourite was the Guardsman sketch, where Jack was a totally incorrectly dressed guardsman standing outside Buckingham Palace and Glen was the bullying sergeant major making his life a misery. Jack liked material that mixed pathos and comedy.

Then of course there was his tap dance, which Jack genuinely learned up a close, and his rendition of 'Susie', a real classic. As he danced Jack would say, 'Stop the band, where the hell are they getting all that music?' when his legs would take him no further.

There are so many other memories . . . the 'Sonny Boy' sketch, when Jack would sit on Johnny Beattie's knee and say, 'this is the only sketch where the wee boy is older than his father.'

We used to do a lovely little girl and boy double, which tagged like this,

Jack: 'My name is Dan and when I grow to be a man, I want to be a missionary and go to Japan if I can, and I think I can . . . thank you.'

Mary: 'My name is Sadie and when I grow to be a lady, I wanna get married and have a baby if I can, and I think I can . . . thank you.'

199

Jack: 'I've changed my plan. I don't want to be a missionary and go to Japan. I'll stay at home and help Sadie with her plan if I can, and I think I can. I'm bloody sure I can.'

What roars of laughter we got with this simple stuff.

In our double act, the gags never changed. As he grew older, Jack liked the true and tried material. For example:

Jack: 'I like your perfume.'

Mary: 'It's called Perhaps.'

Jack: 'How much is it?'

Mary: '£20 a bottle.'

Jack: 'For £20 I wouldn't want Perhaps.'

Mary: 'What would you want?'

. . . and Jack's tag, 'I'd want Sure.'

Little gags of that ilk, always good for a laugh, well told and well worn.

Another nice wee sketch was the comedy policewoman called in to investigate a murder. The scene is girl lying on a couch.

Policewoman: 'What's her name?'

Feed: 'Karen.'

Jack: 'Past carin' she's deid,' then, going to the corpse and examining her nails, 'She's been biting them. She hasn't got a summer season fixed.'

Silly wee things, but they were all Jack's gems. People quote them to me to this day, word for word.

Jack hated rehearsing. We would go to do a one-nighter, sit in the car in complete silence, and two miles from the venue he would say, 'Right, from the top.'

I knew what he meant, the hour-long performance run through to refresh our memories at the last moment.

I wouldn't have dared to say, 'Jack, what are we doing tonight?' I had to wait till he was ready. It was a situation we both understood.

He would spend the first half of his cabaret act taking the

mickey out of me. He'd say, 'Mary used to sing with the big bands. You can still buy her records but only if you've got an HMV record machine and a big dug to bark down the trumpet.' And, 'Mary suffers with arthritis. She's up in the dressing room right now putting Algepan on her legs . . . but don't let her see you sniffing.'

He would go on and on and I'd have to say, 'Please let me on.'

Then I'd say to him, 'Do you play the drums?'

Answer: 'Yes.'

'Well beat it,' and I'd go straight into my song.

In one of the Pavilion shows we had a specialty act, very popular at that time in variety. Gilbert the Chimp was a real chimpanzee, with his human handler. Gilbert did various tricks, stood on a box, stood on his head, his hands, and so on.

Jack was watching from the side one night when Gilbert made a real dive at him. His handler said he shouldn't stand there dressed as a woman but Jack was playing the Dame. He explained that Gilbert loved women, and when there was the possibility of the chorus girls being near him, he would put a bag over Gilbert's head so he wouldn't become disturbed. Anyway, the handler suggested that Jack should visit Gilbert after the show and make up with him. When Jack arrived Gilbert was sitting in the dressing room watching television, with a half pint of beer in his hand, and Jack found himself saying, 'Hello, Gilbert, are you enjoying the TV?'

Jack said he thought he was going mad, but the handler said Gilbert understood what you said. Well he and Jack got friendly, and all was well.

After that, Jack was able to stand and watch his act!

We always had such great laughs together and that's what I miss the most – the fun. All the other things we worry about in our lives like money, success and fame just aren't important. It's family, friends and fun that really make our world go round.

28

FINAL THOUGHTS

It isn't easy to sum up either your life or your married life as you look back over the years. The loss of Jack has been hard to bear and since that we've also now lost his partner and friend Rikki Fulton. I must admit that there are days when I simply cannot accept that both these men are no longer with us.

I don't say that in a trite or superficial way, it is partly because I have never had a taxi ride since without their names coming up in conversation with the driver.

I think, no, in fact I know they will live on long after me and my contemporaries, becoming showbiz legends like Laurel & Hardy or Abbot & Costello – and so they should. I simply could not comprehend that a beautiful, sharp brain like Rikki's could be so cruelly stricken with Alzheimer's Disease. It doesn't bear thinking about.

The first indication I had that this might be so was when I visited the Fulton home one morning, uninvited I must say, to ask Rikki to sign a copy of his autobiography.

Kate was out shopping and Rikki said, 'Come on in, Mary.'

We chatted and he kindly signed his book for my friend. Before I left after our lovely chat together, Rikki said, 'I'll make you a coffee, Mary.'

Now this was a normal happening between two old friends,

but it was so out of character for Rikki. I knew that was always Kate's department, and I felt a little worried. Don't ask me why. But of course in the fullness of time I was proved right, much to my sorrow.

Dear Rikki, it was so unfair.

He and Kate certainly did not have it easy and I was eternally thankful that Jack had escaped it.

Kate and I visited Rikki together when the condition had taken full hold. I must say I would rather have remembered the man as I knew him but I was privileged to be a visitor for only one day.

Rikki died in January 2004 and his funeral was very upsetting for me. It brought back all the sorrow of losing Jack. I asked my son Jim to escort me, and with my friends Carmen Capaldi and Eileen Matthews, we went along to pay our respects. We met up with Johnny Beattie, who was Jack's great friend, and we ended up seated together, as Johnny was on his own.

I was glad when the day was over, I can tell you – too near home for my liking. But you live through these days, as Kate had to do, and try to get on with life, knowing full well that it is a chapter of theatrical history well and truly over. And now, sadly, Kate Fulton has died too.

Ah me, all the 'greats' have gone . . . Jack, Rikki and dear Jimmy Logan.

Not long after I lost Jack, I attended Jimmy's last show at the Pavilion Theatre in Glasgow, a fund raiser for The Maggie Centre, the cancer charity, held shortly before his death in April 2001.

Jimmy came on at the end of the show with his family, his sisters Annie Ross and Heather, and nephew Dominic who had all come over from the States specially to appear in it. It brought back so many good memories for me, especially of Heather, who married Nicky Capaldi, and their son Dominic, who was a wee boy in his mum's dressing room.

Jack and I were topping the bill and the wee soul used to come in to my dressing room and say, 'Auntie Mary, I'm stage daft,' then go down on one knee and sing 'Rockabye Your Baby with a Dixie Melody'. Back then, I knew we had a star on our hands. Dominic is a star in America now, married to Leigh Zimmerman, who is currently appearing in the West End smash hit 'The Producers', Mel Brooks' musical version of his cult movie.

That night at the Pavilion they all sang their hearts out for Jimmy and finished with a number called 'I'm not Waiting to say Goodbye'.

I used to say to him at Show Business Benevolent Fund meetings, 'Sing that wee song to me Jimmy,' and he would reply, 'You mean the one I wrote for my dad?'

Jack Short, his father, asked Jimmy to write a song for his new stage act. Jack was 75 at the time! Watching the video of the show, which came out after Jimmy's death, that song wrenches your heart.

There will never be another Logan Family, let alone another fine all-rounder like Jimmy.

Well, now all that sadness is off my chest, let us move on.

It's no use living in the past. Looking back on it kindly, yes, but not living in it. I've always had a good sense of humour and I think that, more than anything else, keeps you going. There are millions of widows out there so you are not the only one and never forget that, say I. I know I'm getting older but then so is every one else, so the whole universe marches on day by day.

I must say I have found my joy with all my women friends, which has been a pleasant voyage of discovery. I never pegged myself for that because when Jack was living, it was Jack and me together all the time. But I discovered I had been missing out during these years. There is a marvellous camaraderie with widows and those who won't go to their graves wondering. It's a solid thing. They never let you down, give you moral support and company on hospital visits, join you for lunch and a trot round the shops, and are damned good confidantes. My mother's saying about being lucky if you can count on five really good friends remains so true.

Mother really did have some wonderful sayings like, 'He was a gentleman down to his navel,' and her standard reference to any illness, 'It'll take feet, Mary,' always made me imagine, when I was a kid, lots of little feet running about in my tummy then disappearing off down the nearest road.

But back to the present. I have the best fun every Tuesday night. That's my BAFTA evening (British Academy of Film and Television Arts, to give its posh name). I joined three years ago, and as it was new to me, I have found it another interesting avenue. We see all the films before they go on general release.

Alison Forsyth is our Scottish director. She and my good friend Janice Forsyth of BBC Radio Scotland fame, front the evenings and I get to meet straight actors every week. What do I know about acting? The only time I nearly found out was when I was doing a scene with Jack, Elaine C. Smith and James McPherson.

Jack and I played the 'mein hosts' in a bar, and Elaine and James chatted to us.

I do recall thinking they were very casual about it . . . until I saw the show on television. There they were looking very natural, and there was me hopping about like a cat on hot bricks. Nobody told me to be low key, and television is so different from stage work where you have to project. I tell you, I was like a startled prawn.

On the BAFTA nights we often have a question and answer session after the film, when members can have a dialogue with producers and directors, and sometimes members of the cast. They speak a different language from the Scottish variety theatre artist.

I have had my moments at the Bafta, like the night I said to Tam White, the well known Edinburgh blues man, who was in the cast of that night's movie:

'I didn't know you could act Tam,' to which Tam responded, 'I didn't know myself.'

And the director interposed, 'Mary, he was in 'Braveheart' – he's hiding his light behind a bushel.'

My favourite Bafta film of all time is 'Cider House Rules' starring Michael Caine. It's the story of a country doctor who is in charge of an orphanage and helps out young girls who are in trouble. I've hardly missed a film a week for the past three years at Bafta, and that is the one that sticks in my memory.

Sometimes one of our mates has a few lines in the film we are about to see, and we all light up when she comes on the screen . . . yes, it is a lovely fraternity.

As well as our jaunts down south, The Scottish Music Hall and Variety Theatre Society has an annual luncheon, held at the Glasgow Royal Concert Hall. It's always such an enjoyable day, meeting and greeting old pals like Irene Sharp, of the well known singing double act Cormack & Sharp and Helen Randell, a chum of long standing . . . and so many others of the show business fraternity.

Every year a personality is honoured for their contribution to show business. Two years ago, I trotted in for the lunch and did register that most of my family were there – but the penny didn't drop. When the lunch was over, I settled myself comfortably, eager to learn who would be up for the honour this time. The recipient was announced and, glory be, it was Mary Lee!

Billy Differ and Johnny Beattie spoke about me. My dear friend Myra Crichton made the presentation, a beautifully framed montage of photographs of me in my halcyon days with Roy Fox, with the inscription, 'Mary Lee, always a star.'

I tell you, it was enough to bring a tear to a glass eye.

I was so chuffed . . . and it was completely unexpected. I thanked them, did some gags and a few of my one liners from the Aunty Mary Lee show and we all had a good laugh and went home happy . . . well I certainly did.

I think Jack would have been proud of me. I could just hear him saying, 'She does it all herself, you know.'

Life goes on, as we know it must, and to honour his memory, I shall continue to do my own thing till the time comes that I meet up with the other half of the act. But I'm not rushing it!

ONE LINERS

In the old show business tradition, always leave them laughing. Here's a few wee gems from Aggie and I to cheer you up a bit!

My pal Aggie comes from Troon, where the tide has to ask permission to come in, and the seagulls fly upside down, so they'll no make a mess . . . Oh she's VERY pan bread!

We were standing in the rain waiting for a bus. Aggie said: 'Mary, if All Bran makes you regular, why do they no give it to the bus drivers?

See feet – without them you wouldnae have a leg to stand on.

I said, 'Aggie, your hair's turning white.'
She said, 'I know. I've jist been doon to pay my council tax.'

Aggie's jist had plastic surgery – Hughie cut up all her credit cards.

Aggie went into a bank and said, 'I want to open a joint account with someone with money.'

She's going on holiday.
I said, 'Fly Quantas Airlines, Aggie.'
She said, 'I'm no an Australian.'
I said, 'Well I fly Virgin Airlines, and I'm no a very good dancer.'

She said, 'I'd love to go somewhere I've never been.'
I said, 'Try the kitchen.'

Mind you, Aggie's mother was aye in the kitchen. Aggie was 14 before she knew her name wasnae 'Taste that'.

Last year Aggie and I went to Tenerife. The beach was that crowded we ended up in other peoples snaps.

If the woman in front of me hadn't had her ears pierced we'd never have seen the water.

We went to the bingo last night. They shout out the numbers in Spanish so the visitors canny win.

Aggie went for a night out with the girls. She came home and told Hughie, 'I met a fellow who said I've got the cutest nose!'
Hughie said, 'Did he tell you what a fat bum you've got?'
Aggie said, 'No, he never mentioned you.'

Well that was a few funnies for the Christmas Party. As my mother used to say, 'You're just as well laughin' as greetin'.'

There are no prizes for guessing who was the greatest influence on my life – Isa, my mammy. I've still got a little tube of her face cream in a box. It was called Velati. She was some stuff.

Well, this is me since yesterday.

I hope you all live to be a hundred, and I'm the last voice you hear . . . and do remember, it's nice to be important, but it's more important to be nice . . . 'Byee.